Praise for the Book

The author addresses the concept of forgiveness in a clear and concise way. He points out that, as human beings, we need forgiveness from God because of our rebellion and disobedience to His requirements. The beauty of this as pointed out by the author is the free provision of God's forgiveness through Jesus Christ to anyone who would come to God and ask him to forgive. I believe the world would be a different place altogether if the concept of forgiveness can be embraced by the human race. Unforgiveness is one key weapon Satan uses to break relationships especially marriages. Siblings are known to rise up against one another while Nations revenge against each other because of unforgiveness. This is a book every human being, should read and discover the benefits associated with a forgiven life and also the secret of living a life of forgiving others.

Professor Geoffrey Kihara Rurimo
Multimedia University of Kenya

The thrust of this book, as its title indicates, is the practice of forgiveness as expounded in the bible. Drawing from many biblical examples of both Old Testament (OT) and New Testament (NT), it underlines the importance of forgiveness hence the positive effects that arise from the practice of forgiveness. It also shows and thus warns of what could happen when forgiveness is neglected. The examples make its content rich and beautiful because they come from the private and public lives of individuals.

The other beauty of the book lies in its use of free flowing and simple language so that all and sundry can follow the author's thoughts. This should not be construed to mean that it is simplistic in its arguments for indeed it carries a profound message that needs to be heard by all. Its subject is critical in our society where knowingly or unknowingly we seem to offend each other so often and in many places. The offended person will learn godly reasons and practical steps on how to practice forgiveness.

I believe that many people whose thought patterns have acted as strongholds due to un-forgiveness resulting in unresolved issues will be delivered upon practicing what the book teaches. I see restoration of relationships that may have gone bad at family, church, workplace and therefore society as the readers obey the teachings herein. I therefore unreservedly recommend the book for all individual consumers and particularly public ministers such as preachers, counselors etc. The book can also be read profitably as a basis for discussion by small groups.

Rev Dr. Karita Mbagara,
Senior Pastor,
Christ is the Answer Ministries (CITAM) - Woodley

I have enjoyed reading through this book. It is very readable. It's simple language makes it attractive to the reader apart from the fact that the topic is one that most human beings (born again Christian believers & Unbelievers) have to confront at one time or other in their lives. Of course much has been written about forgiveness and sermons delivered from numerous pulpits through the ages. The lives of such world heavy weights as Nelson Mandela, Corrie ten Boom; the fictional character in 'Cry thy Beloved Country' and, to some extent, Mahatma Gandhi all give witness to the power of forgiveness. Despite all this, Forgiveness remains elusive as many of us self-righteously justify charting out paths of unforgiveness.

This piece zeroes in on attitudes and perceptions of many (East) Africans. It carefully examines various situations, justifications and excuses we have /give for NOT forgiving in the light of our Lord Jesus' own experience with his friends and foes. This lays a very strong foundation for the case being made in this piece for forgiving and being forgiven. The writer is at pains to show that all human beings need to receive and give forgiveness. By comparing the nasty experiences in our lives with what Christ went through the reader is left with no excuse to remain unforgiven or unforgiving: our experiences pale into insignificance compared with the horrific scenes of Jesus Christ's earthly life. Jesus' twin command to ask for forgiveness from God (through Him who bore all sin) and to forgive is presented starkly and its negation clearly shown as a one-way ticket to an eternity outside of God's paradise. The writer is appealing to his readers to accept God's forgiveness which is the only guarantee of eternal life. He also appeals to those who, having received God's forgiveness are now in danger of losing it because they will not forgive others!

Esther Womulabira
Intercessor, CITAM - Valley Road

FORGIVENESS UNLIMITED

You Can Be Forgiven
You Can Forgive

IAN OKWADO

WESTBOW
PRESS®
A DIVISION OF THOMAS NELSON
& ZONDERVAN

WestBow Press books may be ordered through booksellers or by contacting:

WestBow Press
A Division of Thomas Nelson & Zondervan
1663 Liberty Drive
Bloomington, IN 47403
www.westbowpress.com
844-714-3454

Scripture quotations marked NLT are taken from the Holy Bible, New Living Translation, Copyright © 1996, 2004, 2015 by Tyndale House Foundation. Used by permission of Tyndale House Publishers, Inc., Carol Stream, Illinois 60188. All rights reserved.

Scripture quotations marked TNIV are taken from the HOLY BIBLE, TODAY'S NEW INTERNATIONAL VERSION®. TNIV®. Copyright © 2001, 2005 by International Bible Society. Used by permission of Zondervan. All rights reserved worldwide.

ISBN: 978-1-6642-2823-8 (sc)
ISBN: 978-1-6642-2824-5 (hc)
ISBN: 978-1-6642-2825-2 (e)

Library of Congress Control Number: 2021905578

Print information available on the last page.

WestBow Press rev. date: 04/06/2021

CONTENTS

APPRECIATION

I sincerely appreciate God the Father who has forgiven me beyond measure, God the Son, who died on the cross to purchase my forgiveness and God the Holy Spirit who prompts and empowers me to forgive at all times.

I also appreciate my dear wife, Florah, with whom we have learnt how to forgive, an unavoidable part and parcel of every marriage relationship. I also appreciate my 4 lovely boys, Ivan, Dan, Alyvin and Anthony, through whom I learnt the art of patience and forgiveness unlimited.

I also appreciate my precious brothers and sisters with whom we have worked together in ministry at the Kenya House of Prayer, Intercessors For Kenya (I4K), CITAM Karen Intercession Team, who have been an eternal blessing to me. Of special mention are Rev Phoebe Mugo, Sister Sharol Githinji, Brother Hudson Bugasu, Pastor Benson Nyang'or, Rev Abok Ager and Professor Geoffrey Kihara.

Special thanks to Sylvia Korir, my true daughter in the Lord, and Pastor Benson Nyang'or, who both took time to read the entire manuscript and offer valuable contributions.

Sister Esther Womulabira and Rev Karita Mbagara also did a tremendous job in reviewing the book and encouraged me on the journey. May the Lord remember their labour of love and grant them their full reward.

FOREWORD

This book is a recommended reading for all. It discusses the need for forgiveness by everyone from the individual level, to family and even at national and international levels. Everyone has need of forgiveness, for all of us are sinners. It also shows us the heart and character of God in forgiving even those who have offended Him the most: Christ forgave those that mocked and crucified Him.

The book paints unforgiveness as a cancer that brings physical illness, as well as social malaise killing our communities and crippling marriages. It shows that divine healing flows through the channel of forgiveness, and if we would only learn to forgive, our healings would follow more easily. It will provoke you in some ways, as the example below shows:

"I know many people are seeking for divine healing but are neglecting the greater gift of forgiveness which is more important. I see it every week in our church. The queue for those seeking forgiveness of their sins is very short and at times has no one, while the one for healing is always overflowing."

The book is written in simple easy to understand language and is rich in scriptural reference. There are prayers included inside to help us put into practice lessons learned. The book can serve as a devotional, with its rich scriptural backing. I recommend it for those in ministry, especially prayer ministers.

Pastor Benson Nyang'or,
Intercessors For Kenya (I4K) Ministry
Nairobi

INTRODUCTION

Those who will find themselves spending eternity in hell will be there simply because they have refused to receive the free gift of forgiveness from God and to render forgiveness to others.

I started on a journey to discover the truth regarding forgiveness in the year 2000 after a preacher from Rwanda visited our church and told us how he went to heaven and during his time there he was also shown what is going on in hell. The worst part of his story was that he saw a born again Christian, a sister whom he knew very well going to hell. On inquiring from the Lord he was told that this sister fell sick and was admitted to hospital for many days. Unfortunately, her pastors, church elders and other believers she expected to visit her in hospital failed to show up for whatever reason.

Remembering all she had done for them, her commitment to church and how she visited the sick and even cleaned those who were totally unable to help themselves, she vowed that she would never forgive them. She died with unforgiveness and therefore booked her eternal destiny in hell. The case of our sister in this story is not an isolated one. Unforgiveness remains one of our greatest challenges in modern times. This is clearly depicted on counseling lines in church. Many of those who come for this noble service are basically dealing with one or other issue caused by unforgiveness.

Through this book you will be able to understand:

1. How you can receive forgiveness unlimited from God for all your sins and book a place for yourself in God's eternal kingdom.

2. Why God wants you to forgive those who have hurt and offended you in the past. It will also transform your mindset on how to deal with people in the future.

3. How you can effectively offer help and support those who are carrying baggages of unforgiveness, hatred and bitterness to lay them down and pick up the yoke of Christ.

I have included Bible verses to ensure that my message remains within the boundaries of God's word. My prayer is that this book will be a blessing to both Christians and non-Christians as the principles drawn from God's word apply and work for the entire human race. Counselors, especially those who deal with matters of relationships will do well to embrace and apply these principles in their daily activities.

CHAPTER 1
IT'S A MAN'S MALADY

To get us started on this topic, we will look briefly at some definitions of forgiveness. This foundation will help us throughout the book as we discuss matters forgiveness.

Forgiveness is the intentional and voluntary process by which an offended person undergoes a change in feelings and attitude regarding an offense, let's go of negative emotions such as vengefulness, with an increased ability to wish the offender well.

Psychologists generally define forgiveness as a conscious, deliberate decision to release feelings of resentment or vengeance toward a person or group who has harmed you, regardless of whether they actually deserve your forgiveness.

Forgiveness enables you to stop blaming or being angry with someone for something that person has done, or not punish them for something

Unforgiveness is a huge burden to carry as we will realize later on. The Lord Jesus offers us a clear way for disposing our unnecessary burdens. *28 Then Jesus said, "Come to me, all of you who are weary and carry heavy burdens, and I will give you rest. 29 Take my yoke upon you. Let me teach you, because I am humble and gentle at heart, and you will find rest for your souls. 30 For my yoke is easy to bear, and the burden I give you is light."*, Matt 11:28-30.

The whole human race has fallen and is in need of forgiveness. In the Garden of Eden, Adam and Eve sinned against God and thereby introduced the rot in the very essence of our nature. This means that every human being irrespective of their upbringing, religion, race, color or status in society, is a sinner in need of forgiveness. Apparently no one is exempted because none is perfect.

Adamic sin affected our whole outlook to life in matters spiritual and natural. Our view of God and fellow man has been grossly deprived. Love for God and our neighbors are the two hinges upon which Christianity rests. It is impossible for anyone who does not love God and his neighbor to be a Christian. Our ability to do this would beget perfect harmony, joy and peace. However, being descendants of Adam, we experience many limitations and end up offending and hurting one another repeatedly. The only rational way out is giving and receiving forgiveness. We are constant offenders to God and man.

God offenders

Despite our 'natural' offense – sin; we often offend God through our disobedience, rebellion and stubbornness. We lay aside God's commands and standards and craft for ourselves human standards. We fail to understand that God has given us His laws, commands and regulations for our own good and that by diligently observing them, our joy will be full. We fail to see that obeying God will give our lives meaning and will make us a blessing to others too.

The scriptures tell us that we *have 'All sinned and come short of God's glory' and it goes on to emphasize that it is '... written, There is none righteous, no, not one...,' Romans 3:10.*

It is sometimes difficult for us mortal men to realize the extent of our weaknesses and sinfulness. Some of our faults are hidden, not just from the public but also from ourselves. David asks God to forgive him his hidden faults and deliver him from deliberate sin which becomes a way of life if not viewed and dealt with according to God's word. He cries; *How can I know all the sins lurking in my heart? Cleanse me from these hidden faults, Ps 19:12-13.*

Humanity has become so blatantly vile that in the human rights circles today the world over, what the word of God categorizes as wickedness such as abortion, sexual perversions including lesbianism and homosexuality are regarded in some places as socially acceptable lifestyles. Biblically, these are clear examples of deliberate sins. The consequences attached to such deliberate sins are spelt out in the scriptures below.

Or do you not know that the unrighteous will not inherit the kingdom of God? Do not be deceived; neither fornicators, nor idolaters, nor adulterers, nor effeminate, nor homosexuals, 10 nor thieves, nor the covetous, nor drunkards, nor revilers, nor swindlers, will inherit the kingdom of God, 1 Cor. 6:9-10.

If any of the items mentioned in this portion of scripture is part of your life, then you need to cut it off immediately if you want to set foot in the New Jerusalem. Remember that with God there is no compromise. You either have to change your ways or abandon any dreams of an eternity in God's Kingdom. Incredibly, I have even come across homosexuals who claim to be born again. That is one of the greatest forms of deception in modern times. There is no way a born again Christian can comfortably engage in homosexuality. In the following scripture, the Bible uses harsh language in describing homosexuality.

That is why God abandoned them to their shameful desires. Even the women turned against the natural way to have sex and instead indulged in sex with each other. And the men, instead of having normal sexual relationships with women, burned with lust for each other. Men did shameful things with other men and, as a result, suffered within themselves the penalty they so richly deserved. When they refused to acknowledge God, he abandoned them to their evil minds and let them do things that should never be done, Rom 1:26-28.

We learn that failure to turn away from our sins including the ones just enumerated will eventually result in our being abandoned by God. It is evident that continuously living a reckless life of sin will result in judgment from God. We need to be careful and always ask God to search our hearts and forgive us even what may not appear as sin in our eyes.

Offenders of humanity

We offend our fellow humans in speech and deed. It is important to note that some offences are deliberate or intentional while others are purely unintentional. The things we say and or do to others may obviously be self-centered and often cause some form of harm including discomfort, shame, disgrace, injury or loss to another person.

Many people wonder how they can know they are in sin. This knowledge comes in two main ways; either our conscience will naturally prick us and lead us into feelings of guilt and remorsefulness or the wrong may be brought to our attention by the aggrieved party. Whichever way, when the matter is brought to our attention, how we react is important to God, to us and those around us. The tragedy here lies in our failure to acknowledge wrongdoing and seek for forgiveness.

In our fallen human nature, it is considered weakness to acknowledge our failure, sin or any form of wrongdoing. In fact we would like to be regarded as perfect, immaculate and incapable of wrongdoing. This is clearly manifested daily in our courts of law. Even though people are forced to swear with the Bible in hand and declare that they will speak the truth, the truth only and nothing but the truth, most of them end up speaking white lies hoping to save themselves in that way. Most of the accused end up pleading not guilty, even when clear evidence is readily available to prove otherwise. This is exactly what Isaiah the prophet was talking about to the people of Jerusalem.

He clearly declares what will eventually happen to all self-righteous people

...You are certain that disaster will spare you when it comes, because you depend on lies and deceit to keep you safe. .. Hailstorms will sweep away all the lies you depend on, and floods will destroy your security. Isa. 28:15-17.

We can confidently lie to men and occasionally get away with it. Usually human judges rely heavily on what is availed to them in terms of evidence to make their rulings. In some cases where the evidence is scanty or insufficient the accused person is set free and goes away celebrating.

However, I think the greatest error we make is to lie to ourselves; when we know in the deepest recesses of our hearts that we are in error or we have offended someone and deliberately fail to make amends. We actually brush it aside as if the event or action never happened. I can promise you that the hailstorm is on the way. It is just a matter of time before your refuge of lies is swept away. God has promised justice in the end.

It is easy for us, when it is still daylight, to accept our positions of failure and seek forgiveness from those we have wronged. In most cases where people have confessed their failures, I have witnessed the offended person being broken down to tears and uttering the all important words in eternity "I forgive you". What a joy this brings into the hearts of both people. Confessions of one's wrong has in the past healed families, restored relationships and even resulted in physical healings. The situation is still the same today.

Remember also that you cannot pray or serve God effectively when you have ignored your offences against others. God, who is perfect and just, will not allow you into His presence. He requires us to sort out matters with our fellow humans before we approach him. This was clearly illustrated by the Lord Jesus.

Matt 5:23-24 admonishes us thus; "So if you are standing before the altar in the Temple, offering a sacrifice to God, and you suddenly remember that someone has something against you, leave your sacrifice there beside the altar. Go and be reconciled to that person. Then come and offer your sacrifice to God."

Clearly, the door to effective prayer remains closed as long as you are aware of someone with some unresolved matters. It is cheaper for you to confront the person and make peace as soon as is practical. The Lord Jesus wants us to live in peace with all men.

Think about it!
"Do you need to confess something to someone today?"

When offended by others

Some people wonder why others do them wrong. It may sound like an overstatement but I say, it might be a strange expectation to expect not to be hurt. As long as we live in this world, someone will offend us. Jesus our master warned us that offenses must come; therefore, we must expect some hard days. You can be a very nice person; doing good things to others and handling them with all the care in the world. You may therefore expect that others will also treat you in the same way. However, it does not always happen this way in real life.

The words of Jesus in Mathew 5:11-12 confirms that you will be insulted, persecuted and be maliciously accused simply because you belong to him. While the words of Jesus are true and eternal, no one would like this kind of thing to happen to them, including myself. But for the many years I have lived in the world, more so as a Christian, I can tell you without blinking that it happens exactly the way the Lord said it. I know in a measure what it means to be insulted, to be cheated and conned and what it feels like to be accused falsely. People can even manufacture and supply imaginary evidence to prove you guilty when you are completely innocent.

I was comforting a sister who was deeply troubled and she had so many questions about her life. She had been hurt on so many different occasions and it seemed like it had now reached a climax. As I opened Matthew 5 and started reading the words of Jesus to her, she collapsed in a heap and sobbed uncontrollably.

These are some of the questions she asked me:

• Why do people treat me like this?

• Why does it always happen to me?

- Why can't people, including born again Christians, just be fair and speak the truth?

The truth is that we will be offended by others, but we must realize that we will also offend others. Some of the most unexpected people will hurt us and become obstacles in our life's journey. I have come across people who have been offended greatly by their loved ones including parents, siblings, close friends and even church leaders.

As I was busy writing this book, one of my sisters in the office gave me an assignment to urgently locate a good church where she could move. To me this seemed a tall order but she claimed that some of the leaders in her church were hypocrites. One of the elders asked her, a married woman, out for a date! She promptly declined. (Oh! Lord give us more of these kind of women in the church). From that time they became enemies and are no longer on talking terms. It is no wonder she is looking for an alternative place of worship. This case is just an example of how an offence can proceed from a spiritual leader.

When we get offended by others, many people wonder if there is a way out of the pain and confusion that results from these encounters. The good news is that there is always a way out. We need to learn to do the right things in these circumstances if healing will be our portion. Christ has a lot to tell us about our reactions and attitude in the day of offense. Consider Matt. 18: 14-18;

"If another believer sins against you, go privately and point out the fault. If the other person listens and confesses it, you have won that person back. But if you are unsuccessful, take one or two others with you and go back again, so that everything you say may be confirmed by two or three witnesses. If that person still refuses to listen, take your case to the church.

If the church decides you are right, but the other person won't accept it, treat that person as a pagan or a corrupt tax collector.

From this text in the gospel of Mathew Jesus also teaches us that the real aim of approaching an offender is not to punish or take revenge, but rather to win the other person back. In a situation where we see a brother or sister falling into sin, we cannot just ignore it since we know the end result of such actions. We can save the situation by confronting the person and helping them understand what their sin is and the available options for restoration. It is a part of our standing Christian responsibility to seek the highest good for our fellow believers and restore them back to the narrow way that leads to eternal life. We are not to destroy but to save and not revenge.

This is in line with the teachings of the Lord Jesus that you should count your suffering as a blessing. Go ahead and bless those who curse you, pray for them and love them. They are actually good human beings being used by the enemy to distract you from the path of faith and obedience to God. Remember that God reserves the right to revenge on your behalf. Do not take that honor upon yourself to try and help Him. The result is likely to be disastrous for you. Rom. 12:19-21 tells us to;

Never take revenge, my friends, but instead let God's anger do it. For the scripture says, I will take revenge, I will pay back, says the Lord." Instead, as the scripture says: "If your enemy is hungry, feed him; if he is thirsty, give him a drink; for by doing this you will make him burn with shame." Do not let evil defeat you; instead, conquer evil with good.

Now you know how to deal with those arrogant people, those who want to take advantage of you and make your life difficult. God has a perfect way of dealing with them. Judgment may not come as swiftly as we may want but it is as sure as sunrise. If you live long enough, you will have time to witness God revenging on your behalf. Be faithful on your part and leave the rest to God. On the other hand remember revenge should not be our main goal. We just release the matter into the hands of God and leave it at that.

A cruel sister is forgiven – A true story from Kenya

I have left this story intact as given to me by a dear sister who went through humiliation. When I informed her that I was writing a book on forgiveness, she asked me to include her story.

My story begins when I stayed with my elder sister who was paying my college fees as my parents were retired and unable to do anything. All household chores were left to me including cooking, cleaning and many other duties she assigned to me like massaging her back. However, with time my sister became extremely verbally abusive towards me and I could not defend myself. I chose to keep quiet in respect for her and for the sake of my college education.

As days passed it got so bad that at one time when my elder sister died, the one she comes after, our relationship took a strange twist. The process of burial took about a week. I had been very close to my late sister. My sister was buried on a Sunday. My sisters and brothers left and went to the various towns where they lived as I chose to stay back and help at the funeral with visitors and to comfort my mother.

After three weeks I returned to Nairobi where I used to reside with my sister. The journey back took about eight hours and it was just two days to Christmas. I was exhausted when I arrived with my luggage at my sister's house. On seeing me she immediately began to abuse me saying that I should not unpack my luggage but return home immediately. Since it was late in the evening, I told her politely I could not travel back home that night. Finally, she allowed me to stay for the night but early the next morning she woke up with much insults and went a step further to throw my things out of the compound. She then commanded me to get out and locked the gate leaving me outside without giving me any money.

I had nowhere to go and the next day was Christmas! During those days cell phones were not common. I had some little money in my pocket so I went to my friend's offices, but found they had already left. However, just when I was giving up and was going to take a bus to go back and wait for my sister to return so that I can see if she had a change of heart, I heard someone call me by my maiden name. I turned round to find my cousin I told her what happened and she said my sister had actually called all my cousins and relatives bragging about the way she threw me out of her house. My cousin sympathized with my situation and invited me to her house where I stayed with her during the Christmas holidays and had a good time with her family. As the New Year began my cousin advised me to go back to my sister and act as though the whole episode never happened and she said 'act as a fool'. I did exactly that and went on to stay with my sister. Apparently she accepted me back though we did not discuss the past incidents. Somehow, she started feeling guilty and she began to buy me clothes or treat me better.

However, as for me the pain of what she did over the years and how abusive she had become began to wear me out and I started crying secretly, I had low self-esteem and became generally withdrawn. A few years later, I went to a prayer meeting, in those days it was called 'wailing womens' meeting. The Pastor's wife was ministering on offences and harboring unforgiveness. As she began to speak I found myself weeping uncontrollably. She then called everyone who had been offended by someone close to them to go forward. I went and the strangest thing she said was that you need to go to the person who wronged you and forgive them.

At that point I thought God is very cruel, I am the victim, I have been a victim of my sister's cruelty for years, she is the one who should come to me not me to her. The minister went on to say you should leave your gift at the altar and go forgive your sister! I cried for two days and nights thinking and planning how to visit my sister.

When I finally went to my sister's place, where I had to take two buses, I found her at home and she thought I had come to beg for something, so she was rude and arrogant with me and said she is too busy if it is food I want I can go to the kitchen and serve myself whatever is left and then leave her house. Since I was tired, I ate the food and as soon as she noticed I was through she told me to get out of her house. As I left the house, she closed the gate and I stood outside the gate but I could not leave. I just stood there and told her that the reason I came was to tell her that I loved her and that I had forgiven her for all the past issues. Immediately, I felt something lift off of my shoulder and tears of relief flowed freely. When I turned to look at my sister from the holes on the gate she was also weeping. She could not believe that I had forgiven her. I left that place a better person. I consequently got a good job after that, things opened up in my life and since then my sister has treated me with respect.

Prayer:

My Father in heaven, please reveal to me instances in my life where I have failed to forgive men and where I have been disobedient, rebellious and stubborn. Forgive me for this terrible wickedness I entertained and help me to overcome all these and to return back to the pathway of obedience. I now choose to consciously and unconditionally forgive everyone who has wronged me and ask you to forgive them also. Help me to forget all the wrongs done to me and to love the offenders according to your commands. Release me from the prison of Unforgiveness. From today, I pray for your grace to unconditionally forgive all who will wrong me in future whether they ask for forgiveness or not. Let all the doors that have been locked against me due to Unforgiveness be opened now. Help me to recover all I have lost during the period I allowed Unforgiveness in my life.

CHAPTER 2
THE FORGIVING GOD

This section will bring you to a position where you can receive forgiveness, unlimited from God. If you have been walking about with a guilty conscience, because of your actions and even considered yourself ineligible to receive forgiveness, you will find hope here and guidance on what you can do, as is clearly revealed in the Holy Scriptures. I assure you that your life will experience a total and eternal transformation.

Invitation to receive Forgiveness, Unlimited

God introduces Himself in scripture as a forgiver. He shared with Moses his curriculum vitae (CV) or resume. This introduction is the hope to which every human being can cling on and ask for forgiveness. It is among the most amazing and incredible sections in the Bible.

5 Then the LORD came down in a cloud and stood there with him; and he called out his own name, Yahweh.[a] 6 The LORD passed in front of Moses, calling out,

"Yahweh![b] The LORD!
   The God of compassion and mercy!
I am slow to anger
   and filled with unfailing love and faithfulness.
[7] I lavish unfailing love to a thousand generations.[c]
   I forgive iniquity, rebellion, and sin.
But I do not excuse the guilty.
   I lay the sins of the parents upon their children and grandchildren;
the entire family is affected—
   even children in the third and fourth generations."

Dealing with our own guilt from sin is quite a challenge to humanity. We struggle and often wonder if we can come to a place of peace with God. The good news is that God is the author of forgiveness. It is extremely important for you to understand that the Almighty God, your creator, has taken the initiative to invite you for forgiveness. This is actually the most important invitation you will ever receive in your lifetime. Your eternal destiny is entirely dependent on your personal response to this invite. No one else in the world can respond to it on your behalf. The bible says;

"Come now, let's settle this," says the Lord. "Though your sins are like scarlet, I will make them as white as snow. Though they are red like crimson, I will make them as white as wool. 19 If you will only obey me, you will have plenty to eat. Isa. 1:18-19.

It would take a very careless person to ignore or fail to show up for such an important appointment. Take the case of someone who is about to be convicted in a court of law. He seems to have no way out since all the evidence against him is available both in court and in the public domain. He then gets an invitation from the president or prime minister of his country to go and attend a discussion session and explore a way out of the quagmire. Under some circumstances, only a presidential pardon can save such a person. Otherwise, after conviction, the person would be taken straight to the gallows. One would be unwise in every sense of the word to ignore such an important appointment as it may actually spell the difference between life and death.

In a similar manner, God has made an open invitation to every human being. Remember that you do not have to commit sin to become a sinner, you are born a sinner. That is why no one needs to teach you how to steal or lie, it just happens automatically. For that very reason, the sentence of death hangs over our lives as stated in Romans 5:12 and 6:23 respectively;

Sin came into the world through one man, and his sin brought death with it. As a result, death has spread to the whole human race because everyone has sinned…For the wages of sin is death, but the free gift of God is eternal life through Christ Jesus our Lord.

We have all sinned. My friend it does not help matters to try and justify our personal positions. Some of us, graduates of the debating club, would have a rough time taking this position lying down. However, just know that all our human arguments will not change anything. The word of God is forever settled in heaven and His laws apply to all people irrespective of their background, color, status, religion or beliefs. As long as you are a human being, descended from Adam, you are a sinner by nature and in dire need of a savior.

On the other hand when we look critically at our past, we might be tempted to feel that we are beyond forgiveness. Yes, indeed you would be beyond it, if the assessment was being done by human beings. If a committee was to be formed, which would select people who qualify for forgiveness, clearly your name may never make it into the list. However, God's take is totally different: even if the color of your sins is scarlet or red like crimson, you remain a candidate for forgiveness. Do not disqualify yourself and neither can anyone disqualify you. Look at the following examples of people who were in similar desperate situations like yours and how God dealt with their cases. They had reached what we commonly refer to as the end of the road. There was no more hope for them, their end had come.

How does God actually forgive sin?

Isaiah 43:25

> "I—yes, I alone—will blot out your sins for my
> own sake and will never think of them again.

The woman caught in the act of Adultery

John 8:2-11 paints quite an unbelievable scenario. This is the story of the woman caught in the very act of adultery. Just picture that nameless woman, and the crowd. We are not even told whether she was dressed up fully or halfway as she was frog marched straight from the bed to the place of instant and final judgment. The law demanded that she must be stoned to death. Worse still, it was the religious leaders and Pharisees, experts in law who were on the frontline accusing her. The fitting punishment according to the law needed to be applied in this case and Jesus better just authorize this or so they thought. The media was ready with cameras, to capture yet another episode fitting for a breaking news item. They brought her to Jesus, who is the owner of the law. Even though it is commonly referred to as the Law of Moses, we all know that it was God's law.

However, the response from the Lord here was totally unexpected and seemed to be out of context. It is the words of Jesus softly and clearly spoken to the woman on the death row, that gives hope to every sinner, whether you have been caught red handed in the act or not. The Lord forgave her all her sins instantly and unconditionally.

John 8:10-11

10 Then Jesus stood up again and said to the woman, "Where are your accusers? Didn't even one of them condemn you?"

11 "No, Lord," she said.

And Jesus said, "Neither do I. Go and sin no more."

The greatest lesson we learn from this encounter is that you can be forgiven today, unconditionally. I am very sure that woman, considered more sinful than others in the society, began a brand new life and went home praising God. All her sins, including adultery were forgiven and erased forever in an instant. Everything changed in her life in an instant. She had been glaring at the darkness ahead. Actually, death was imminent and unavoidable, but God rescued her. That is one of the reasons why Jesus came, to save you from your sins and set you free from its bondage and consequences. This is what I call forgiveness, unlimited. No sin is too small or too big for the savior. Just bring it and lay it at His feet. You will be forever grateful that you did.

The Robber on the cross

The second example is found at the cross. This one is even more amazing. The Lord Jesus hung on the cross and was in terrible pain. Two criminals hang there with him, one on His left and the other on His right. It was just a matter of time before all of them died. The sentence of death had been issued and appropriate action taken to ensure the world was rid of these criminals in the most painful way possible; crucifixion! Of course Jesus was innocent, but because He had ruffled feathers in the religious circles and fallen out with the political leadership of the day, He also faced the same consequences. Luke 23:39-43 gives us a glimpse into a conversation that went on between the criminals and Jesus:

"So you're the Messiah, are you? Prove it by saving yourself and us, too, while you're at it!" But the other criminal protested, "Don't you fear God even when you are dying? We deserve to die for our evil deeds, but this man hasn't done anything wrong." Then he said, "Jesus, remember me when you come into your Kingdom." And Jesus replied, "I assure you, today you will be with me in paradise.

I have read this passage in the scriptures several times and it has never stopped amazing me. In my own human wisdom, I don't see why the fellow should be forgiven at all. The man was a criminal by profession. He lived by the gun, robbing people, raping women and even killing those who resisted him. He had been tried in a court of law and found guilty. Evidence concerning his criminal record was availed and he was found guilty. In fact, he himself pleads guilty in his conversation with the fellow criminal on the cross. Why on earth should such a fellow be considered for forgiveness? Besides, of what use is he to the kingdom even if he is born again at this point. He is going to die anyway, in a few hours or minutes. He is on his deathbed with no hope of ever being rescued, no mercy in sight, only death in view.

However, God's attitude and reaction is just the exact opposite of what a man would do. Verse 43 gives us this answer;

'And Jesus replied, "I assure you, today you will be with me in paradise.'

Please note that the Lord did not take time to consider and review the request. No commission was established to look into the request and provide a report of findings. The response was spontaneous: Today you will be with me in paradise. This is forgiveness, unlimited. And it is extremely good news for you and me. Today your life can be changed dramatically and eternally. Even if it is your last day on the earth, or your last hour, there is hope. All you need, like the criminal, is to approach the Lord and ask for forgiveness. The Lord Jesus has not changed as confirmed in Hebrews 13:8 which declares that, *'Jesus Christ is the same yesterday, today, and forever.'*

The same answer Jesus gave to the criminal during his last moments on earth can be yours today. Forgiveness is an already packaged gift from God. All that is required of you is to accept it. The decision to accept the gift is entirely yours as an individual. Of course friends and parents may play their part in trying to convince you to accept the gift but the final responsibility lies in your hands.

In a certain church where I was invited to minister some time ago, a pastor had been transferred from that congregation to another one outside the city. Immediately after his move to the new destination, his former congregation decided to prepare a farewell party and bought a wonderful gift for their pastor. Unfortunately, the pastor never turned up for the farewell party. The congregation waited in vain on the appointed day and then finally placed the gift in a safe place hoping that he would turn up later and pick it. One year down the line they were still holding the gift in safe custody and the former pastor was not showing any signs of coming for it. The new pastor tasked himself to call him from time to time until he gave up. They ended up giving the gift to one of their elders who was retiring since the rightful owner failed to accept it.

Today you have an opportunity to accept a gift from God, the one who loves you with an undying love. Jesus is the one who died in your place on the cross. He suffered on your behalf. He paid the full price for your redemption and forgiveness. You don't need to improve your life. You don't have to pay anything. You don't have to subject yourself to any form of suffering to qualify for forgiveness. All that is required of you is to ask for this unlimited forgiveness and receive it. Will you accept it? Or will you remain in your sins? The choice, my friend, is yours. Don't behave like the pastor who refused a free gift from a church. My prayer is that today will mark a turning point in your life.

Think about it!
Will you respond to God's invitation, or just remain
stubborn and continue living in your sins?

Sample Prayer For Salvation

Dear God, I acknowledge that I am a sinner in need of your saving grace. I realize that I cannot help myself. Thank you for sending Jesus to die for me on the cross. Forgive me all my sins and wash me with the precious blood of your son Jesus. I choose to follow you and obey your commands from now on. Teach me your ways and connect me with other Christians who will support me to grow into a strong believer. Help me to remain faithful to you until the second coming of your son. I ask this in the name of the Lord Jesus Christ, Amen.

CHAPTER 3
MAN CAN FORGIVE YOU

Man has great God given capacity to forgive his fellow man. Some people say they cannot forgive because of their view of the weight of the wrong done to them. Others say they can forgive but not forget.

The Bible is rich in wonderful and sweet accounts of people who forgave and were forgiven by others. They will offer answers to those who swear they cannot forgive others. Some people in the bible had to forgive in circumstances that appear incredible and in matters you might consider unforgivable. This means we can forgive beyond the limits the worldly standards would brand as impossible.

David and Saul

There are many biblical accounts on forgiveness but the case between David and Saul is a classic. Saul, a man from the tribe of Benjamin, was anointed by the prophet Samuel to become the first king of Israel. This was something that he had not thought possible all his life neither was it part of his ambitions; even in his wildest dreams. However, God just chose him as king and therefore his fate was sealed.

Saul received the kingdom on a silver platter, no effort from his side. He did not have to go through a campaign, prepare a manifesto, and or join a popular political party. According to his records and existing reality, his tribe was the smallest in Israel and his family the least important in that tribe. But that did not matter to God, what he required is the right man for the right job. It was such a humbling experience, too good to be true; Saul even hid himself. It took God, to reveal where the man was hiding.

Saul was anointed king and began to rule. He scored a number of victories in his first few years of service before pride, arrogance and disobedience caught up with him. This became his undoing and continued until God rejected him completely and chose someone else to take his place as shown by 1 Sam 15:10-11…

"I regret that I have made Saul king, for he has turned back from following Me and has not carried out My commands." And Samuel was distressed and cried out to the LORD all night.

Saul literally turned away from God, prompting his replacement with a man after God's own heart. You will need to check out your heart today and find out if you are still following the Lord or if you have forsaken Him like Saul. As I keep on saying, let us learn from the mistakes of those who have gone ahead of us. Should we reject God's word, we can be sure that God will also reject us.

The Lord watched His prophet agonize over the failure of the King he anointed. God spoke to Samuel and said; *"How long will you go on grieving over Saul? I have rejected him as king of Israel. But now get some olive oil and go to Bethlehem, to a man named Jesse, because I have chosen one of his sons to be king." 1 Sam 16:1*

And in 1 Sam 16:12-, Samuel the prophet of God anointed a young man from the house of Jesse.

So Jesse sent for him. He was a handsome, healthy young man, and his eyes sparkled. The LORD said to Samuel, "This is the one—anoint him!" Samuel took the olive oil and anointed David in front of his brothers. Immediately the spirit of the LORD took control of David and was with him from that day on. Then Samuel returned to Ramah.

It is interesting to note that this anointing ceremony was performed behind Saul's back. Being a wicked man, as revealed in his later endeavors', even Samuel was afraid of him. Afterwards, David joined Saul's service both as a musician and a soldier. God used his praise and worship skills to drive away the demons which were disturbing king Saul.

Soon, Saul's love for David died. Love turned into hatred on the same day David killed Goliath; an arch enemy of Israel. What was supposed to be celebrated in Israel as one of the greatest days of victory turned to be the beginning of darkness for King Saul.

Saul turns against David

The scriptures says;

It happened as they were coming, when David returned from killing the Philistine, that the women came out of all the cities of Israel, singing and dancing, to meet King Saul, with tambourines, with joy and with musical instruments. The women sang as they played, and said, "Saul has slain his thousands, And David his ten thousands." Then Saul became very angry, for this saying displeased him; and he said, "They have ascribed to

David ten thousands, but to me they have ascribed thousands. Now what more can he have but the kingdom?" Saul looked at David with suspicion from that day on. 1 Sam 18:6-9

Surely, no one can blame the women for singing the way they did. It is one of those things that come out naturally especially in times of great victory over the enemy. Even to this day, whenever we have celebrations the women, and men, still sing using the available facts on the subject matter. But for Saul this was like a great insult. His pride could not allow him to swallow such. He came out with a master plan to deal with David conclusively.

Now it came about on the next day that an evil spirit from God came mightily upon Saul, and he raved in the midst of the house, while David was playing the harp with his hand, as usual; and a spear was in Saul's hand. Saul hurled the spear for he thought, "I will pin David to the wall." But David escaped from his presence twice, 1 Sam 18:10-11.

Saul took the law into his own hands and was determined to eliminate David. However, God protected David and saved him from Saul's maneuvers. Saul actually hunted down David, he sent men of war to look for him, set up spies across the country and did everything in his power to try and destroy him. His mind was already made up. David had to die as soon as possible. This was the kings top most priority over all else that was happening in Israel. And Saul even tried to make it everyone's responsibility to accomplish this task.

As time went on, Saul went on rampage, killing anyone he suspected to be a friend or accomplice of David. He was so reckless in his mission that he slaughtered eighty five priests of God at Nob. (1 Sam 22:18-20). Saul was angry with everyone, including God and he was not going to rest until his arch enemy, David was eliminated from the face of the earth.

The fury of Saul against David was evident everywhere he went. At one point, he almost killed his own son, Jonathan for talking positively about David. Can you imagine what level of hatred this was? And for what reason?

Hatred can lead someone to great and incredible heights of wickedness. Don't allow any amount of hatred to dwell within your heart. Pray continually that God may search your heart and deliver you from every form and appearance of hatred. Surely you don't want to be like Saul, who killed anointed priests of the Most High God, their wives and little ones, just because he thought they had supported David in a way.

Think about it!
What is your reaction when you meet someone who deeply admires some qualities in your enemy? The enemy could be a political leader, a boss in the workplace, a certain preacher or even as close as a parent or sibling.

David refuses to revenge

To make the long story short, David managed to get some golden opportunities to take revenge against Saul but he restrained himself from killing him. His servants on some occasions urged him to kill Saul. At times they even invoked the name of the Lord; seeing it as a God given opportunity to kill Saul.

David responded that he could not assault one on whom the anointing of the God of Israel had once rested. He could not allow himself to touch the Lord's anointed. Apparently, God's anointing was not nullified by Saul's disobedience. This is an invaluable lesson to us Christians today. We need to tread carefully when dealing with servants of God. Even when they are on the wrong, we have a responsibility to help restore them back to God's path of righteousness and also to continually pray for them. We should not make it our ambition to kill and finish them off especially if we get the opportunity. David knew one truth; that God Himself knows how to deal with His anointed servants.

Saul went on his self-destructive rampage ending with his death at the battle on Mt. Gilboa where he and Jonathan his son died. Instead of David throwing a party to celebrate, he weeps and even orders the killing of the one who took it upon himself to bring him the news of Saul's death.

David and his men tore their clothes in sorrow when they heard the news. They mourned and wept and fasted all day for Saul and his son Jonathan, and for the LORD's army and the nation of Israel, because so many had died that day, 2 Sam 1:11-12

I often wonder what I would have done was I in David's shoes; Most probably I would have held a grand party to celebrate the departure of a sworn enemy. Not so with David. He and his men mourned, they wept and fasted the whole day. David even composed a song of lament for Saul and Jonathan.

Then David said to the young man who had brought the news, "Where are you from?" And he replied, "I am a foreigner, an Amalekite, who lives in your land." "Were you not afraid to kill the LORD's anointed one?" David asked. Then David said to one of his men, "Kill him!" So the man thrust his sword into the Amalekite and killed him, 2 Sam 1:13-15.

Not only did David mourn for Saul, but the man who confessed to having assisted Saul to commit suicide at Saul's request was also killed. Soon after Saul's death Abner, who had been the commander of Saul's army, organized a quick swearing in ceremony and proclaimed Ishbosheth son of Saul the new king over Israel. Meanwhile David was sworn in as king over Judah.

Immediately war broke out between Israel and Judah in which many people were killed.

David's Army was led by Joab while Ishbosheth's army commander was Abner. Later when Abner was murdered by Joab, David ordered his men to mourn for him. He was one that had stood with the anointed king of Israel and severally in obedience to God's word, had lead Israel's army to many victories. David knew this and understood that those who had gone before him had to be honoured. However, the most notable action David took was to receive Saul's grandson (Jonathan's son), Memphibosheth, to eat at his table.

David's response to Saul's descendants is what I call Forgiveness-Unlimited. If David, a normal human being could forgive to this extent, you can also do it. Ask for grace from God, not just to forgive your enemies, but also to show them favour and kindness. This is the only way they will know you are truly a son of the Most High God. Our Christianity should not just be displayed in word, but also in deed. After all, they say actions speak louder than words.

I have walked with you through the story of David because of it's value when it comes to the beauty and weight of the message of forgiveness, but the Old testament is littered with other worthy stories. Jacob and Esau, Joseph and his brothers and the many events that God forgave his children Israel and brought them back to himself.

Turning to The New Testament, forgiveness is a constant theme. I have already referred to the story of the 'Woman caught in the very act of adultery.' The account detailing the experiences of the prodigal son and his father is another true example of forgiveness unlimited.

Jesus Himself came preaching the good news to the poor. He forgave those who were in need of forgiveness for their sins. Oh! The joy experienced by those who were forgiven.

Paul and the other writers of the Pastoral letters carried on the forgiveness tone in their letters. Paul constantly seeks to compel his readers to seek and receive forgiveness from the Lord and one another.

When people live in one house or are married, they will surely offend one another. A husband will wrong his wife and vice versa Brother and sister will fight, even though they are of the same blood.

People will always offend and be offended by others. Why do people find it so difficult to dispense forgiveness? Let's peek into this matter now and I hope we may understand the heart of man.

A rapist is forgiven

I encountered a young lady who had gone through a terrible rape experience earlier in her life. It was so painful for her that she had not revealed the matter to anyone except her one time boyfriend. During our initial interactions, I had spoken to her very strongly about 'forgiveness unlimited' as outlined in scripture. She confirmed to me that she had forgiven all those who had wronged her in the past. And as if that was not enough, she called the rapist in a restaurant and bought him a cup of coffee and forgave the man. This was more than 10 years after the ordeal.

Even though the man has never apologized for his actions, and is living and acting as if nothing ever happened, my sister has since moved on with her life, having forgiven him in full as commanded in God's word. She no longer feels the pain, anger or bitterness and it's no wonder she could afford to buy for him a cup of coffee. I hope that the sister's action will cause the man to turn over his life to God one day. Obviously if he doesn't, his reward is on the way, and may not be very far off.

Think about it!
There are people who may have hurt you terribly in the past. What are you going to do as proof that you have truly forgiven them from the heart? Pray and ask God for direction.

CHAPTER 4
SOME REASONS WHY PEOPLE HARBOR UNFORGIVENESS

1. Racism and or tribalism

Racism is enmity between two or more races for example the Caucasians and the people of African descent. It can also be hatred between tribes for –example in Africa where there many tribes; the Kikuyus of Kenya may not like the Zulus of South Africa. Hatred may be resulting from historical actions which took place long before we were born. In fact by the time we arrived on this planet and learnt how to distinguish good from evil, our parents or relatives may have already inducted us into the realm of Unforgiveness by speaking negatively about a certain person, family or community. They teach you how to hate them naturally and most of the time without a reason until it seems there are justifiable grounds to withhold forgiveness. It may also be due to old injustices that were not dealt with and in which forgiveness was withheld or never asked for, so we have a situation where 'old unforgiveness begets present unforgiveness.

Tribalism has been institutionalized in different countries, especially in Africa. Christians and some servants of God have, on some occasions been used by the enemy as advertising agents of the vice. Unfortunately, it does not augur well with many if you try to explain that discriminating other tribes, races or people groups and looking at them as second or third class citizens in their own country is a grave sin before the creator who made them in His own image. In God's eyes, it does not really matter whether the hatred is directed towards an individual, a group of people, a particular community or race, the end result is the same.

The results of ancient hatred are manifested in unending tribal wars and hostilities. Many people have lost their lives and properties on the altars of tribal hatred. Others have lost their standing in God by submitting themselves to the evil spirits of hatred.

This kind of hatred can only be addressed by Jer. 32:26-28 where; … *the LORD declares; "I am the LORD, the God of all the peoples of the world…*

It is important to note that our God does not show favoritism to any one tribe or community above another. Let us all consider the following;

- We are all created by God, to glorify His name on the face of the earth.

- All believers are washed with the same blood; the precious blood of Jesus.

- All believers are sons of God and no one group or community is accorded special privileges in the kingdom.

- The New Jerusalem will be composed of people from every nation, tribe, people and language. These will be your next door neighbors throughout eternity. It is profitable for us to start learning how to live with them early enough.

God commands us to distance ourselves from every form of hatred. We will do well to pray and ask God to deliver us from this kind of bondage. It is up to us to choose whether to hate people or forgive and love them because the death penalty hangs over those who embrace a permanent stand of hatred and unforgiveness.

Think about it!
Never let anyone recruit you to hate someone
who has never wronged you!

2. Perfectionism (Self-righteousness)

Even though we are all imperfect humans, perfectionists believe that mistakes must never be made and that the highest standards of performance must be achieved. They are a brand of human beings who feel they are extraordinary. They cannot even excuse themselves for doing wrong let alone excuse the faults of others. They see the faults of others as contradictory to the standards they have set for themselves. I met a young lady whom I believe falls in this category. She was complaining about something I had asked her to forgive and forget. She told me flatly, that she does not forgive anything as a matter of principle. At least she is not born again and has no regard for God's word, therefore I understood her.

I also remember a difficult husband and wife situation that left me thinking a lot about perfectionism. A wife and a husband were having trouble in their relationship. The wife reported the matter to her pastor prompting the pastor and a church elder to visit the home with the intention of brokering peace. They were welcomed by the couple and sat down. Immediately the husband went into the bedroom and came back with a notebook. In this notebook were written all the mistakes and errors attributed to the wife from the day they got married. The record was up to date and had details including the date, the time and nature of offence. After showing the visitors these records, he paused and asked them "how would you expect me to forgive such a person?" With such hard evidence on record the church men had an uphill task convincing the man to forgive his wife. The husband did not see his side of the coin. His wife was always the one on the wrong from the day they got married he kept updated and detailed records of offences.

Woe unto you if you happen to get a perfectionist as your boss, wife or husband. Your troubles will be many. You will never seem to get anything right. There will always be shortfalls on your side and a lot of room for improvement.

Much will be required from you. Conversely, all they do is meticulous, beyond any degree of error. As I have said before, perfectionists hardly forgive. They just don't see the sense in forgiving. They would rather write you off and end the relationship than forgive. But just what does the Bible say about this?

You must make allowance for each other's faults and forgive the person who offends you. Remember, the Lord forgave you, so you must forgive others, Col. 3:12-14

You must make an allowance for other people's faults. No human being is perfect. Those who have attempted to look for Mr. Right or Miss. Right as lifetime partners have always been disappointed because these people do not exist on earth. And even when they think they have finally landed on the right person and get married, they eventually find fault and many of these relationships end up in divorce.

When you remember how the Lord forgave you, you are able to forgive others in the same way. God did not demand perfection from you, why should you expect it from others?

3. Pride

Some people are too proud to forgive. The reason they give is that forgiving makes them look weak. They feel they are being taken advantage of and must always stay on top by withholding forgiveness. Listen to what someone who was not even a Christian had to say about this matter.

The weak can never forgive. Forgiveness is the attribute of the strong. Mahatma Gandhi 1

The Lord Jesus has directed us to be like children. In fact He said that the kingdom of God belongs to those who are like children. When you spank a child, he forgets very fast and continues to deal with you as if nothing ever happened. To be like a child means you have to humble yourself and let go.

You younger men, likewise, be subject to your elders; and all of you, clothe yourselves with humility toward one another, for GOD IS OPPOSED TO THE PROUD, BUT GIVES GRACE TO THE HUMBLE, 1 Peter 5:5. (Emphasis added)

For the proud, I can see only one thing, clearly your fall is imminent if you don't change your ways. God himself is against the proud. How will you make it in life if God is against you? Pray that God will deliver you from every form of pride.

4. Revenge Factor

There are some people who feel that when they are wronged they must revenge. They reason that the other person has to pay for their mistakes. They must learn the lesson otherwise if they get away with it they might repeat the error. For example if a spouse has cheated on you, they will advise you to cheat on them also. Now we all know that two wrongs do not make a right and revenge only makes a bad situation worse.

The word of God guides us on what we should do.

"Never take revenge, my friends, but instead let God's anger do it...," Rom 12:19-21. Instead, as the scripture says: "If your enemy is hungry, feed him; if he is thirsty, give him a drink; for by doing this you will make him burn with shame. "Do not let evil defeat you; instead, conquer evil with good.

Do not allow revenge to be your standard response to offenses. Each one of us is responsible for our actions before God who judges and punishes all forms of disobedience. No human being can escape God's judgment, great or small. When we know this, we allow God to revenge on our behalf. On the contrary, seek opportunities to treat your offenders well.

Some time back, I advised a brother who was being mistreated by his boss to take him out for lunch and speak to him kindly. This is God's standard. If you get a chance, then use it to show love to the one who is against you. This is your heavenly calling and it works wonders. You conquer evil by doing good and in that case provide room for God to judge righteously. The Lord Jesus also spoke about this to His disciples

38You have heard that it was said, 'An eye for an eye, and a tooth for a tooth.' 39 But now I tell you: do not take revenge on someone who wrongs

you. If anyone slaps you on the right cheek, let him slap your left cheek too. And if someone takes you to court to sue you for your shirt, let him have your coat as well. 41 And if one of the occupation troops forces you to carry his pack one mile, carry it two miles, Matt 5:38-41.

This text summarizes what God expects from a believer. Do not take revenge. It is the wrong, ungodly way of dealing with those who offend you. Obey God and you will reap the rewards.

As Josh Billings rightly said "There is no revenge so complete as forgiveness".

5. Unresolved Anger and Bitterness

Unresolved anger is something to be dreaded by all people. One never knows when it's going to rear its ugly head, who it's going to victimize, and what price the perpetrator may be forced to pay as a result of the damage he causes.

It is true that any believer harboring unresolved anger in his heart is keeping a ticking time bomb capable of doing a lot of damage to a great many people. What's worse, sometimes it's all done in the name of the Lord Jesus Christ. James discusses this fact in his epistle,

Remember this, my dear brothers! Everyone must be quick to listen, but slow to speak and slow to become angry. Man's anger does not achieve God's righteous purpose, James 1:19-21.

Slowness to become angry is a virtue we should all ask of the Lord. I have come across people who tolerate/endure insults, mistreatment to an extent they look very abnormal. But it is good to remember that a true Christian lives on a plane/level that is higher than that of a non-Christian. Your boss at work could do something to irritate you only to discover that you have not reacted negatively and even still speak kindly to him without showing any sign of anger or bitterness. That is the true fruit of transformation. It is an indication that you are already dead and that Christ is the one who lives in you. This kind of endurance can cause a non-believer to rethink their position and even consider giving their lives to Christ.

Anger could be justified because of offenses perpetrated against us or could even be caused by our own misconceptions and used by the enemy as an avenue to cause strife and division in the family, church or community. Hebrews 12:15 says,

"Looking diligently lest any root of bitterness springing up trouble you."

The phrase 'looking diligently' comes from the Greek word episkopos, which means to supervise, oversee, and correct. So you are the overseer of your heart. Each day you must monitor, direct and correct what goes on there. You can't blame your bad attitude, resentment and unforgiveness on others. You are responsible!

When somebody offends you, it's up to you whether or not you let bitterness take root. You can't control what other people do, but it's the 'inside' part - the part you can control - that God holds us accountable for. You get to decide whether or not irritation turns into anger, anger into resentment, and resentment into retaliation.

The reason weeds take over a garden is because the gardener doesn't pull them up fast enough. When your garden is choked by weeds you can't say, 'I don't know how it happened!' When you are 'looking diligently' you will see them moving in. The only way to stay free of the weeds the enemy wants to sow in your life is to be attentive to the condition of your heart. When you're faced with a hurtful, offensive situation, refuse to let a wrong attitude take root and produce bad fruit. Instead, ask God to help you replace those destructive thoughts with mercy and forgiveness towards the people who hurt you. The Bible says,

'Above all else, guard your heart, for it is the wellspring of life'. Proverbs 4:23.

You may actually have very valid reasons to be angry with someone or some people. Just have a look at the following scenarios which present themselves as excellent opportunities for harboring permanent hatred and bitterness:

- You may have been wronged by your husband, wife or child. I know of husbands who have walked away from their families for no apparent reason and with no intention of ever returning. I also know of wives who have walked out of their marriages leaving their husbands and children stranded.

- You may have been mistreated by parents or even abandoned to die for one reason or another. Some children have been abandoned due to a kind of disability.

- Your parents may have rejected the spouse of your choice and refused to attend you wedding or send you gifts. They could have cut off ties with you, labeling you a rebellious child and an outcast.

- People known to you may have killed your parents and left you an orphan with no means of survival.

- You could have been uprooted from your home and sent into a refugee camp due to political or other reasons.

- You may have suffered in the hands of cattle rustlers, gangsters or carjackers.

- You may have been raped by a friend, relative or an unknown person.

- Your friends may have abandoned you in your hour of need and failed to help you even when they had the ability and resources.

- Your boss may have denied you the much deserved promotion or the promised salary hike.

- You may have lost an election or a nomination position through an unfair process.

- A good brother or sister may have borrowed your money and failed to pay, to pay at the agreed time or even refused to pay back.

- A lover may have broken your heart by walking out of your life just before the wedding, or on the wedding day.

All the above and many other similar situations in life are not easy to deal with. If we apply human wisdom in these cases, none of those people deserves any mercy or forgiveness. And from a legal perspective, they do not qualify to be forgiven unless and until they have paid for the wrongs in some way.

You may be tormented from time to time with bad thoughts and may even be tempted to contemplate suicide. Whatever your lot in life, I pray for you today, that God will give you the ability to get rid of your anger and bitterness. The simple reason is that harboring anger and bitterness will not help make the situation better nor will it resolve the problem. It may actually work on you like cancer and kill you in the long run. That is an unnecessary and untimely death which you should not allow to happen to you.

Prayer

Please consider Psalm 103:8 as you prepare to pray:

The LORD is compassionate and merciful, slow to get angry and filled with unfailing love.

You may wish to bring to mind any relationships where you need to exercise patience, such as with your family, children, marriage or at work. Then slowly make the following prayer:-

Lord Jesus, may I be slow to anger and filled with true love for my neighbor

I know I'm going to need Your help here, because if I try to go solo on this I'll fail for sure

Please fill my heart with compassion and patience

May I be ready and willing at all times to forgive - myself and others

Not just this once, but as many times as it takes

Thank you that you are forever giving, when it comes to forgiveness

Please fill my heart with understanding, may I always seek to contemplate

What somebody may be suffering before I jump to any conclusions

Because I know that you never cease, to pardon me

Lord, may I be slow to anger and filled with love

Because you are my hero, and I'm following You

In Jesus name, Amen

CHAPTER 5
FORGIVENESS UNLIMITED &
THE FORGIVENESS OF OUR SINS

Looking at the teachings of the Lord Jesus Christ on forgiveness to His disciples, it imparts a whole new dimension on what God requires of us as His children in this area. I pray that as you read, your mind will be renewed and your attitude transformed to fit into God's perfect will.

I guess many of us went through tutorials in our churches before either baptism or confirmation. We therefore know the Lord's Prayer like the back of our hands. In some churches the Lord's Prayer is part of the Sunday service and many recite it probably without taking into account the weight of the words they speak out. Let's do a quick review.

Forgive us the wrongs we have done, as we forgive the wrongs that others have done to us, Matt 6:12.

These are the words of the Lord Jesus as He responded to a request from the disciples to teach them how to pray. A critical assessment here reveals that forgiveness must be part and parcel of us. It must be our permanent companion in life as our guarantee to be forgiven by God is purely hinged on our willingness and obedience to forgive others. We are therefore forgiven as we forgive. In other words, when we fail to forgive, we should not expect to be forgiven. In fact the Lord continued to emphasize this point in the following verses.

"If you forgive others the wrongs they have done to you, your Father in heaven will also forgive you. But if you do not forgive others, then your Father will not forgive the wrongs you have done", Matt 6:14-15.

We have a choice to make today, whether we want our sins to be forgiven, and that we do by forgiving others. If we fail to do this, we continue to actively involve ourselves in religious activities but without the hope of ever accessing the presence of God.

Many people in our generation, including well meaning Christians, are still walking around with a huge baggage of past hurts, anger and bitterness. They consider themselves to have been wronged beyond measure and therefore unable to forgive. They can even ask you "how do you expect me to forgive him after all he has done to me and especially because he did it deliberately and intentionally to hurt me?" They may even think that the Lord does not understand the magnitude of their suffering. Otherwise if He did, he may probably have put terms and conditions to this command, allowing circumstances under which forgiveness should be granted or withheld from offenders.

However, for us to understand the Lord's position and fully accept it, we will need to look at some other scriptures from Isaiah the prophet.

8 "My thoughts are nothing like your thoughts," says the Lord. "And my ways are far beyond anything you could imagine. 9 For just as the heavens

are higher than the earth, so my ways are higher than your ways and my
thoughts higher than your thoughts., Isa 55:8-9.

The ways of God are not our ways. Our human ways and thoughts
are so limited that we cannot comprehend some of the commands
the Lord gave us. Our honorable responsibility is basically to
obey like soldiers in the army. One thing a soldier will never do
is to argue with the commander, simply because the commander
most likely has a much broader view of the battle front and is
implementing the best strategy for the moment. Actually, failure
to obey the commander can lead to judgment in a court martial
or worse still to death in the hands of the enemy.

I remember when I went to the District officers' office in search
of registration for an Identification card, an administration
policeman in full uniform reported on duty while I was there. It
became apparent that there was a problem between him and his
boss. The man was ordered to run around the office a number of
times. He obeyed without a word while dressed in his military
boots and full uniform and kept running round for no apparent
reason until he completed the specified rounds. I found that quite
ridiculous. How can a full grown African man, with a wife and
children, obey a command to run around in full view of the
public? In fact I did not ever imagine becoming a member of
the disciplined forces. But the key word for that kind of career is
obedience.

Failure to obey, as I mentioned before can lead to severe
consequences including dismissal from the force.

Why should we as soldiers of the Lord believe that things are
any different in His army? The fact is that Unforgiveness has
the potential to lock heaven's gates against us. More so for us
who are intercessors, and are constantly knocking on the doors

of heaven, we cannot afford to walk in Unforgiveness. I have heard several stories about Christians who landed in hell because of Unforgiveness. We need to take these words with the weight given by our eternal king, the Lord Jesus Christ. We must obey without applying our human reasoning and excuses. The fact that God commands us to forgive means that he has built in us the capacity to forgive and forget.

1 Sam 15:22-23 says;

But Samuel replied, "What is more pleasing to the LORD: your burnt offerings and sacrifices or your obedience to his voice? Obedience is far better than sacrifice. Listening to him is much better than offering the fat of rams. Rebellion is as bad as the sin of witchcraft, and stubbornness is as bad as worshiping idols. So because you have rejected the word of the LORD, he has rejected you from being king.

From this true story, Saul rebelled against God by failing to obey and instead chose the path of stubbornness. He thought he knew better than God and chose to do things his way. In the end God rejected him and appointed David to become king in his place. It is again clear from the scriptures that our God has not changed His mode of operation and will apply the same standards even today.

Forgiveness of sins and physical healing

There is a covenant relationship between forgiveness of sins and healing. I have seen a lot of emphasis being placed on physical healing in some churches with less emphasis on forgiveness. In the story of the paralytic Jesus Christ gives us a fitting pattern of things. Consider these bible verses;

1"Several days later Jesus returned to Capernaum, and the news of his arrival spread quickly through the town. Soon the house where he was staying was so packed with visitors that there wasn't room for one more person, not even outside the door. And he preached the word to them. Four men arrived carrying a paralyzed man on a mat. 4 They couldn't get to Jesus through the crowd, so they dug through the clay roof above his head. Then they lowered the sick man on his mat, right down in front of Jesus. Seeing their faith, Jesus said to the paralyzed man, "My son, your sins are forgiven," Mark 2:1-5.

This is another amazing account in scripture. I don't think there is any other more dramatic like this one. This was a man who was paralyzed and as days passed he was nearing the gates of death. His condition deteriorated so badly that his friends decided to take him to Jesus as a last resort. Someone must have informed them that Jesus had a solution to this problem.

We are not even told where they came from or how far they had walked. But their behavior proves that they were not going to be stopped by anything, including the crowd. They brought the dying man to Jesus through a hole in the roof of the house. When Jesus saw their determination, and the paralyzed man he was also amazed. The first words to come out of His mouth were: *"My son, your sins are forgiven."*

The paralyzed man had all along thought that his main problem in life was this terrible sickness, but Jesus knew that he needed more than healing. Forgiveness of sins guarantees one a place in the New Jerusalem while physical healing is profitable only in this world. You will note that the paralytic did not ask for forgiveness. I don't think he was strong enough to even talk, but at least he could hear clearly. Of course, after granting forgiveness for his sins in the presence of the opposition, the Lord healed him and the man went home praising God to the amazement of onlookers. Jesus forgave his sins first then physical healing followed.

The Bible says that God, 'forgives all my sins and heals all my diseases' (Psalms 103:3). I know many people are seeking for divine healing but neglecting the greater gift of forgiveness which is more important. I see it every week in our church. The queue for those seeking forgiveness of their sins is very short and at times has no one, while the one for healing is always overflowing. I have made it a standard procedure in ministry to first ask sick people whether they want to receive Christ before we pray for healing. In most occasions they say yes, but in some instances they refuse saying they need time to think about it. I still pray for healing on both occasions.

However, I know that those whose sins have been forgiven are in a better position, in that, should they not recover from the sick bed, they will be ushered into Abraham's bosom like Lazarus. Conversely, those who reject salvation, should they die in that condition, will find themselves in hell just like the rich man. Forgiveness of sin is important but we must also consider the place of forgiveness of those who have hurt us and healing.

In John chapter five, we are introduced to a sad story of a man who had been sick and paralyzed for more than 38 years. I say this because he confessed that he had been lying by the poolside awaiting his golden moment for a continuous period of 38 years. I can only imagine what that means. When Jesus found him, he healed him promptly and commanded the man to carry his mat and go home to his family. This caused an uproar in the religious circles of the day and the man was being questioned why he was carrying a mat on the Sabbath day. But when he came across Jesus later, the Lord gave him just one message:"

Go and sin no more or else something worse might happen to you". John 5:11

You need to understand that Jesus was not just on a campaign trail to increase the number of His followers, but rather, he was communicating an important and eternal spiritual principle. Anyone living in sin is susceptible to attacks from the enemy because sin is an open door which gives him a foothold in our lives, a platform to steal, kill and destroy. When a person is healed and continues in sin, he can invite a more serious attack from the enemy's camp leaving him in a worse condition. This principle is made clearer in the following verses:

When an evil spirit goes out of a person, it travels over dry country looking for a place to rest. If it can't find one, it says to itself, 'I will go back to my house.' 25 So it goes back and finds the house clean and all fixed up. 26 Then it goes out and brings seven other spirits even worse than itself, and they come and live there. So when it is all over, that person is in worse shape than he was at the beginning." Luke 11:24-26

I am not at all saying that we should not pray for sick people who are non-believers, but rather that we should encourage them to fortify their lives by surrendering to God fully to ensure the enemy does not visit them again with seven other demons. God is willing; He is prepared and ready to forgive your sins right now. Will you give Him your life?

Forgiveness unlimited–Seventy times seven shall we forgive.

Matthew 18:21-22

21 Then Peter came to him and asked, "Lord, how often should I forgive someone[a] who sins against me? Seven times?"

²² *"No, not seven times," Jesus replied, "but seventy times seven!*

The disciples marveled at Jesus' teaching on forgiveness in Matthew 18. They really wanted to know from Him how many times they should forgive those who hurt them. He had a surprise for them and to their amazement; He commanded that they forgive infinitely. Ah! Their jaws dropped. The disciples must have felt that their master's teaching disadvantaged the offended.

This wasn't strange because as God, Jesus knew that the Father had forgiven the children of Israel numerous times in their wilderness journey. The power of example is probably the greatest learning opportunity we have at our disposal.

Children learn a lot from their parents, not through words as much as through their own examples. It is actually easier to teach students through practical lessons than theory. As children of God we do well to learn how to forgive by looking at how our Father does it.

While God manifested himself through signs, wonders and miracles, the Israelites remained stubborn and stiff-necked. Their journey to the Promised Land was constantly punctuated by murmurings, grumblings, complaints and outright disobedience. They complained about water, meat, manna (food cooked in heaven), their leaders whom God had given them and just about everything else. Sometimes the complaints were so serious that the whole community- men, women and children were weeping at the entrance to their tents.

The history of the desert trek was filled with victories against their enemies, but they displayed the fact that they had no faith to believe God would deliver them in future. It looks ridiculous now but it is a real picture of how we behave before our God. What we learn is that human beings have not changed and they continue until today to murmur, grumble, complain and disobey God in an even greater measure. Pray yourself out of this company.

Let us see the Lord's reaction and consequences of disobedience. Numbers 14:11-12 tells us how God decided to destroy the whole nation by a plague but verses 13-19 reveals how Moses pleaded for the people and the Lord wonderfully forgave them.

'The Lord is slow to anger…forgiving every kind of sin and rebellion'

This happened over and over again. The Hebrews sinned and God forgave them in much mercy, every time they repented and asked for forgiveness.

Think about a people who reject their living God for an idol? They wanted a god they could see and touch and therefore made a golden calf. This was during the period of forty days when Moses went up into the mountain to receive the Ten Commandments. The whole congregation of Israel contributed generously by providing gold earrings, the wealth God had given them in Egypt for an evil purpose. You can imagine this level of rebellion and wickedness.

"So all the people took off their gold earrings and brought them to Aaron. He took the earrings, melted them, poured the gold into a mold, and made a gold bull-calf. The people said, "Israel, this is our god, who led us out of Egypt!" Then Aaron built an altar in front of the gold bull-calf and announced, "Tomorrow there will be a festival to honor the LORD." Early the next morning they brought some animals to burn as sacrifices and others to eat as fellowship offerings. The people sat down to a feast, which turned into an orgy of drinking and sex", Ex 32:3-6.

Sincerely speaking, if God's ways were the ways of man, not one of these people would have remained alive to tell the story. They rebelled against God, made their own god of gold and started to offer sacrifices in total disregard to God's command: *"You must not have any other god but me and "You must not commit adultery.(Exodus 20:3,14)* This is just unbelievable.

Again God was about to destroy the nation he had delivered out of Egypt. It was a nation constantly rebelling and rejecting God and His standards. Moses had to intervene and cry out to God on their behalf; and God forgave them again. It is as if God did not want Moses to intervene but he did anyway and saved the situation. The results of his hearty intercession were recorded in Ex 32:14,

So the LORD withdrew his threat and didn't bring against his people the disaster he had threatened.

Though they did not even seek for forgiveness, their God acted mercifully. They were happy in their orgies and without a care in the world. You understand by now that we are serving a forgiving God. If they could commit this kind of sin against the Most High God, they can and will certainly sin against you. We likewise must learn how to forgive seventy times seven. This is what I call Forgiveness, Unlimited.

Sin's Lifespan.

The story of the city of Nineveh gives us interesting facts about sin/wickedness and God's response. Sin has a lifespan. It grows until it cannot grow anymore. It is as if God says, your sin cannot continue any longer and pronounces His judgment. The scripture says that in the days of ignorance God overlooked, but after knowledge/light came, He commands all men to repent.

According to history, Nineveh was an ancient Assyrian city on the eastern bank of the Tigris River, and capital of the Neo-Assyrian Empire. It was the largest city in the world for some fifty years. It is also recorded that Nineveh was an important junction for commercial routes crossing the Tigris. Occupying a central position on the great highway between the Mediterranean Sea and the Indian Ocean, thus uniting the East and the West, it received wealth from many sources, so that it became one of the greatest of all the region's ancient cities, and the capital of the Neo-Assyrian Empire.

It was to this great city that the Prophet Jonah, a true prophet of God, was sent. His mission as defined by God, was simple and straight forward. He was to announce God's judgment on the City because of its wickedness. God spoke clearly to Jonah;

Now the word of the LORD came unto Jonah the son of Amittai, saying, Arise, go to Nineveh, that great city, and cry against it; for their wickedness is come up before me, Jonah 1:1-2.

There is a period within which God allows men to continue in their wickedness without intervention. This causes some to imagine that God winks on wickedness and that there is no punishment for evil deeds. While they know very well that whatever they are doing is extremely evil and unacceptable they not only continue in the same path (stealing, killing and destroying) but they encourage their friends and relatives to do the same. When wickedness reaches a breaking point God sends swift Judgement. He said of Nineveh that its wickedness has come up before Him. Can you imagine? The stench of Nineveh's wickedness went up until it reached heaven. It became unbearable and intolerable. Something had to be done swiftly. That is why God sent his servant Jonah to declare a forty days moratorium.

Does God measure wickedness? It looks like the answer is in the affirmative. I am not sure what instrument is used to gauge it all, but it seems there is a way God measures these things. During the covenant making process with Abraham, God revealed that the sin of the Amorites had not yet reached its full measure.

Consider this; In the fourth generation your descendants will come back here, for the sin of the Amorites has not yet reached its full measure, Gen 15:13-16.

The Amorites sin was great but it had not yet filled the 'container'. But our God, who knows the end from the beginning, was sure to punish the Amorites, at the right time.

The scriptures we have just refereed to provide evidence that sin, evil and wickedness are measured, and when the 'container' is full, God unleashes His judgement. The other city in which we see the same principle being applied in the Bible is Sodom.

Look at what Gen 18:20-21says:

So the LORD told Abraham, "I have heard that the people of Sodom and Gomorrah are extremely evil, and that everything they do is wicked. I am going down to see whether or not these reports are true. Then I will know."

Now we realize that our sins can be so many and so grievous that God would actually come down to have a closer look and confirm the true state of affairs. Indeed for Sodom and Gomorrah, their sins had reached the full measure i.e. filled whatever 'container' used for measurement and judgement was swiftly announced by the angels who were sent there. It was a very sad and sudden ending for these two cities.

Gen 19:23-25 records:

Then the LORD rained down fire and burning sulfur from the heavens on Sodom and Gomorrah He utterly destroyed them, along with the other cities and villages of the plain, eliminating all life—people, plants, and animals alike.

The cities were full of immorality. Human rights activists had managed to change laws and constitutions so that same sex marriages and relationships were now fully legalized. Not only did they practice these abominable activities among themselves, they also ensured that anybody who visited the city was duly inducted into the process. For those who tried to refuse, force and mob justice were activated to ensure that they complied with the laws of the land. Even though Abraham pleaded with God for the two cities, only Lot and his family were saved. God carried out the judgment as announced by the angels and they became history.

We must understand that we cannot continue in sin forever. The Lord shall surely judge all wickedness and none of us is exempt. The only thing we need to always deeply ponder is that when the Lord hits back it is with such finality that there is no recourse. We need to come out of our sin early. Impunity doesn't help and shall surely be judged.

The judgement of God can be directed towards an individual, a family, community or nation. Repentance is required at all these levels to avert the inescapable divine punishment. The last, final and most painful punishment will be the lake of fire, which was created for the devil and his angels, but to which all unrepentant sinners will also be partakers.

Prayer assignment:

If you are following me carefully, I am sure you can now start relating to some of the movements which are gaining momentum around the world in the name of human rights. They advocate a deliberate departure from God's laws including abortion, same sex marriages and the like.

God has not changed and unfortunately for some and fortunately for others, He is the same yesterday today and forever. I am sure that we are going to see massive judgments from God in our generation. Nations, however small or great, will be judged for deliberately choosing to disobey God. Pray that God will give you a genuine burden to pray for your family, community or nation so they can turn away from idolatry, rebellion and wickedness to start obeying and serving the living God.

CHAPTER 6
FORGIVENESS UNLIMITED
& THE YEAR OF JUBILEE

The year of Jubilee was an appointed feast of the Lord, and probably the most important in the calendar of Israel. It was a Sabbath of Sabbaths and was to be celebrated by all Israel. It was a year of forgiveness and the shofar was to be blown on the Day of Atonement to proclaim liberty across the land. The details about Jubilee are revealed in Leviticus 25. The Sabbath year was also designated officially by the Lord as the year of cancelling debts as per the passages from Deuteronomy 15.

The Year for Cancelling Debts

At the end of every seventh year you must cancel your debts, Deut 15:1-2.

God commanded the Israelites to cancel debts at the end of every seven years. It is important to note that cancelling of debts was not a humble request from God but rather a command. I understand from military sources that when a command is issued, you are on the safe side obeying the command however irrational it may sound. Remember that we are all soldiers in the army of the

Lord and therefore we are expected to obey and carry out all His commands. The scriptures declare that believers in Christ are actually soldiers.

It takes someone who is truly and completely submitted to the Lord, a soldier, to accept all His commands and regulations without questioning. As a matter of fact, we don't have options since obedience in the Kingdom of God is the first cardinal rule.

One thing you will notice in Lev. 25 is that there was no lower or upper limit as to how much debt could be cancelled or in other words forgiven. God deliberately omitted the limits and this means that all amounts owed had to be cancelled unconditionally during the Sabbath year. This is Forgiveness, Unlimited.

The debtor did not have to make an application for the debt to be cancelled. Neither, was anyone required to sit down and consider the reasons why the debt remained outstanding, that is, whether the debtor was actually unable to pay or had simply refused to pay. It was a blanket or mass cancellation of debts.

I met a sister in the church who had once taken a bank loan to bail out her own blood brother who was in financial distress. Her brother finally recovered financially and even started buying new cars, a sign that he had actually come out of his financial wilderness. The interesting thing is that he promptly forgot to repay his sister who had helped him in the hour of need. He even refused to discuss the subject and went on living his life as if nothing ever happened. The aggrieved sister was asking me what she should do.

I advised her to forgive and forget. It was a huge sum of money, but that does not matter, God requires that you forgive unconditionally, cancel the debt and let the debtor know that the matter has been settled for ever and the accounting books closed.

I know when you are reading this, you may respond like some people did to Jesus when they said: This is a hard saying, who can hear it? Deut 15:2 asserts:

This is how it must be done. Creditors must cancel the loans they have made to their fellow Israelites. They must not demand payment from their neighbors or relatives, for the LORD's time of release has arrived.

The big question remains; why should we cancel debts? The answer is simple; because the Lord's time of cancelling debts has been proclaimed. The year of Jubilee is the Sabbath of Sabbaths, that is, the 49th year. On the 10th day of the 7th month, the trumpet was blown across the land to declare the jubilee. On this day God forgave Israel all their sins and literally ushered the nation into a new beginning, a fresh start. What a wonderful thing for the nation? It would of course not be a new beginning for those who were indebted, prompting the command to cancel all debts. Remember that God's forgiveness to Israel was unconditional. It did not matter what level of disobedience or rebellion the people of Israel had displayed, it was time for forgiveness, and they received it on the Day of Atonement, if they followed God's instructions. Following in God's footsteps they were also required to forgive their fellow brothers and allow them to enjoy a fresh start.

Cancelling of debts was to be spontaneous and unconditional. No one was allowed to present excuses as to why he does not want to cancel the debt.

God in His eternal wisdom knew beforehand that some people will borrow and then for one reason or another fail to repay the debt on time or even to repay completely. For those of us who are so blest with material wealth, we look at these scriptures and wonder why God gave this kind of command. And some of the questions running through our minds will be as follows:

- After all, the borrower promised to pay and possibly even signed a commitment on how the repayments would be done easily over a period of time.

- If he knew he was not going to pay, why did he borrow in the first place?

- Why can't he just become organized and pay up?

- Surely he cannot claim to be a Christian when he is not able to pay his debts.

I must confess here that God has allowed me to be in debt for a period long enough for me to learn the lesson in full. I consider that my own personal mistakes led me into the situation and I reached a point where there was no way out. The more I tried to solve the problem, the deeper I sunk into debt until I almost despaired in life. Actually, I was on the verge of giving up ministry as nothing seemed to be working. I prayed, I fasted, I sought for counsel and help from friends and relatives, but life continued to become even harder. I suffered shame, was insulted, despised, threatened and dishonoured for a long time. Finally, the Lord intervened in my life, as He always does when we have reached the end of ourselves. He enabled me to repay all my debts and it happened during the year of Jubilee celebrations in Kenya.

Now I understand and appreciate God's command for cancelling of debts. Although my debts were not cancelled, God made a way out for me according to the proclamation of liberty in the year of Jubilee. This relief also provided means to have the 1ˢᵗ edition of this book published for the glory of our God. I know what it means to be in the prison of debt and the level of desperation people feel when all their means for repaying debts have failed seven times. The Lord Jesus knows and understands our predicament. That is why He issued a command that we should forgive and cancel debts. The Lord took this discussion a notch higher in Deut 15:7-11:

"But if there are any poor people in your towns when you arrive in the land the LORD your God is giving you, do not be hard-hearted or tight-fisted toward them. Instead, be generous and lend them whatever they need. Do not be mean-spirited and refuse someone a loan because the year of release is close at hand. If you refuse to make the loan and the needy person cries out to the LORD, you will be considered guilty of sin. 10 Give freely without begrudging it, and the LORD your God will bless you in everything you do. There will always be some among you who are poor. That is why I am commanding you to share your resources freely with the poor and with other Israelites in need."

God is aware that there are people who will borrow from you and possibly fail to repay. It may already have happened to you. It has happened to me, not once. This is not reason enough for you to carry a painful burden throughout life cursing them. It is a God given opportunity for you to obey His command and cancel the debt. This action does not just release your debtor, but also frees you from the prison of unforgiveness, which as I described earlier, can eternally lock you out of the Kingdom of heaven. If you have such a situation in your life, please take action today and cancel the debts of your brother or sister. Let them know you have done it out of your fear and reverence for God and resume normal relations as soon as possible.

We are also commanded to give generously and without a grudging heart, because when we obey this command then the Lord will bless us beyond our wildest imaginations. And we are also warned against refusing to lend to the poor simply because we don't trust them, or maybe because our past records indicate that they are unfaithful in repaying debts. By the way, you should not even be keeping such records in your archives, simply because they will not help you in any way and also because people change, especially when they have a relationship with God. Apparently, when you refuse to help a needy person and he cries out to God, then you should anticipate some trouble or punishment from God. The same word was repeated by the Lord Jesus Christ in Matt 5:41-42.

When someone asks you for something, give it to him; when someone wants to borrow something, lend it to him,

Being kind to someone in need has benefits we may not know. Once you receive this revelation, you would gladly lend knowing that your action is validated by God's Word and that He will bless you. For instance look at the scripture references below and pray that God will open your spiritual eyes to allow you understand fully:

If you help the poor, you are lending to the LORD—and he will repay you! Prov 19:17.

Are you interested in lending God something? If the answer is yes, then be gracious and open handed towards the poor. You will have lent to the Lord and He promises to repay you back. He will definitely do it, possibly not through the same poor person, but you can be sure of repayment because it is impossible for God to lie or default. And when he repays, it will come with other benefits which you did not expect e.g. good health.

Oh, the joys of those who are kind to the poor. The LORD rescues them in times of trouble. The LORD protects them and keeps them alive. He gives them prosperity and rescues them from their enemies. The LORD nurses them when they are sick and eases their pain and discomfort, Ps 41:1-3.

The promises in Psalms 41 are related to lending to the poor. I know there are many people in this world who would wish, if it were possible to trade in their vast estates in exchange for good health. I have seen many rich people in this world dying from terminal illnesses as doctors were unable to help them. Now that you know the secret, go and share the eternal truths with those who are still alive. Also, apply these values in your own life and you will come out rejoicing with a new testimony. For your information, God is unusually close to the poor, orphans, widows and the underprivileged. He takes great interest in their welfare. Be very careful how you deal with them.

We are also admonished to do good to our brothers and sisters whenever we get a window of opportunity.

9So don't get tired of doing what is good. Don't get discouraged and give up, for we will reap a harvest of blessing at the appropriate time. 10 Whenever we have the opportunity, we should do good to everyone, especially to our Christian brothers and sisters, Gal 6:9-10.

Make it a deliberate policy in your life to do good to all people. God has promised us a rich harvest if we don't get weary; especially when it appears that your good is repaid back with evil. When we obey God, eventually He will repay us beyond our wildest expectations. The area of lending and giving is a fertile ground for planting good deeds. You can try God in this area and I assure you that you will never be disappointed.

Why you should pay off debts

Make every effort to pay off all your debts. On the other hand, we should not use the provisions of the word of God to defraud or mistreat our fellow brothers and sisters. Therefore, whenever we borrow, we should repay promptly to avoid bringing the name of the Lord into disrepute. Rom 13:8 says;

Pay all your debts, except the debt of love for others. You can never finish paying that! If you love your neighbour, you will fulfil all the requirements of God's law.

We are admonished to promptly repay all our debts except the debt of love. Debts keep you in bondage and hinder you from making substantial progress in different areas of your life. Don't wait for your debts to be cancelled, they might not be depending on whom or where you borrowed from. Ask God today to give you the ability to repay all your debts in full. He did it for me and will do it for you also. Remember that with God, all things are possible.

Let us not be like the prophet who died with debts and left problems with his wife and children. Trust God to live within your means and avoid unnecessary debts. For example it is not prudent to walk around with eight credit cards. You may just be setting the stage for your own destruction. The interest charges alone could be sufficient to make you bankrupt.

Let us trust God to be lenders and not borrowers. This is the perfect will of God for us as revealed in Deut 15:6

The LORD your God will bless you as he has promised. You will lend money to many nations but will never need to borrow! You will rule many nations, but they will not rule over you!

God has promised to bless us and make us lenders. This is your portion as a son of God. Pray and declare this scripture over your life. Even if you are beginning from a negative position, God is not limited. He will make a way for you where there is no way and you will soon be a lender.

Some Effects Of Unforgiveness On The Church

God expects the church to lead the way in showing the world how to forgive and forget from the heart. However, due to ignorance or just disobedience, we still find traces of unforgiveness within the church whose effects include the following:

Church divisions

We have seen several churches breaking into factions simply because someone has been offended in a way by the pastor or someone in leadership. I remember one episode when a pastor was to be transferred from one congregation to another. There was such acrimony that the congregation engaged in physical warfare which left many hurt and others admitted in hospital with serious injuries. The ousted faction, after recovery, decided to start a separate church in the neighborhood. Surely whatever wrong had been done was not beyond forgiveness.

Ineffective ministry

When there are divisions amongst the leaders or members of a church, this is sufficient to hinder the church from growing and achieving its God given mandate in a locality. It is clear from scripture that God commands His blessing where there is unity.

1 Behold, how good and how pleasant it is for brethren to dwell together in unity! It is like the precious ointment upon the head, that ran down upon the beard, even Aaron's beard: that went down to the skirts of his garments; 3 As the dew of Hermon, and as the dew that descended upon the mountains of Zion: for there the LORD commanded the blessing, even life for evermore, Ps 133

The enemy uses unforgiveness to try and block the blessing of God from flowing into a particular congregation. Don't give him a foothold in your church. Also it is important to note that many people are visiting churches looking for freedom and answers to their life problems, but far too often our internal conflicts are drowning out the message of grace. They hear us talking about the Prince of Peace, but are they seeing the evidence of His peace in how we relate to one another? What inquirers really want to know is: "If forgiveness is such a wonderful thing, why aren't you doing it?" Our lack of forgiveness hinders to a great measure our ability to share the Gospel message.

Divorce and Separation

The unwillingness to forgive is one of the major causes of marriage breakdown. Unforgiveness is actually the deadliest marriage killing poison used by the enemy to destroy marriages. It is clearly the major cause of divorce and separation of married couples around the world.

Every marriage is made up of two humans with natural weaknesses and strengths. Therefore, anyone who enters marriage should do so with the readiness to forgive repeatedly for life. Your spouse comes with a 100% guarantee that they will hurt and disappoint you at some point. None of us is an angel or perfect, however beautiful or handsome.

It's important to always remember that regardless of how loving your spouse is, he or she will disappoint you, guaranteed. Regardless of how loving you are, you will unintentionally hurt, frustrate and disappoint your spouse repeatedly. Therefore, whoever is unwilling to forgive is not ready for marriage. Every spouse should be a forgiver by default. Live your life with the readiness to forgive (Eph 4:32)

Ephesians 4:32 - Instead, be kind to each other, tenderhearted, forgiving one another, just as God through Christ has forgiven you.

While divorce and separation were seldom heard of or even mentioned in Church in past generations, these days we have an increasing number of Christians who are leaving their spouses. They walk out of their marriages with a variety of reasons. Clearly, as Jesus said, it was not so from the beginning. God's intention is that marriages should last until "death do us part".

You should make efforts to unshackle your marriage from past issues. It is not possible to achieve your marriage destiny by looking backwards. Train your heart to forgive your spouse even when you don't feel like forgiving. You will never forgive if you wait until it feels right. God's grace is given to those who least deserve it. As believers in Christ we enjoy that divine nature with its unique forgiving abilities (2 Pet 1:4). Learn to forgive and see your marriage move on from strength to strength. I have counseled several couples on the verge of divorce. Some we literally intercepted enroute to the divorce court. When the cases were brought to me I wondered at first whether there was any hope in these relationships. But as I spoke to them showing them the way of forgiveness through the word of God, the results are amazingly beautiful and beyond description. I prescribe forgiveness as an essential part of every marriage.

God not only expects us to forgive, but also wants us to forget the wrong and move on to new levels of love and relationship. There are some husbands and wives who are prone to reminding each other of their past mistakes whenever something happens. There's no way they can develop a good relationship if they keep on doing that. As God's children with His DNA in us we must follow his footsteps in forgiving and forgetting (Heb 8:12).

Think about it:
Is there hope for my marriage? Can marriage work
in our day? The answer is YES. Take time and pray
that your marriage will fulfill God's agenda and you
will be a role model in the contemporary society.

Separation from fellowship

Some believers, due to unforgiveness, have separated themselves and refuse to attend fellowship or be associated with other Christians. They have purposed to attend church services on Sunday only, and not be involved in serving or home cell groups. This kind of approach serves to weaken the believer as God never created us to be islands. We need fellowship with one another, just like the first church in the book of acts and also in obedience to the command in the word of God that we should not give up meeting together to encourage each other as we see the day of Christ approaching (Heb 10:25).

The church is also known as the body of Christ and the word of God tells us that every individual believer is a part of the body. It's not possible for the body to function well without all the parts, because it would be disabled. Each one of us has something to contribute in the body. Do not fail to fulfil your prophetic destiny due to offences. There are many who are looking up to you and who will be blessed when you serve in your rightful position.

Sickness

Unforgiveness is the single most popular poison that the enemy uses against God's people, and it is one of the deadliest poisons a person can take spiritually. It causes everything from mental depression, to health problems such as ulcers, cancer and arthritis. This does not mean that every single case of cancer, is due to unforgiveness, but I am saying that it can cause cancer. Cancer comes from the devil, scientist can't explain it, doctors don't understand where it comes from; it's the symptoms of a curse. God allowed the Israelites to face diseases and sickness when they disobeyed Him.

"If you refuse to obey all the terms of this law that are written in this book, and if you do not fear the glorious and awesome name of the LORD your God, then the LORD will overwhelm both you and your children with indescribable plagues. These plagues will be intense and without relief, making you miserable and unbearably sick. He will bring against you all the diseases of Egypt that you feared so much, and they will claim you. The LORD will bring against you every sickness and plague there is, even those not mentioned in this Book of the Law, until you are destroyed, Deut 28:58-61.

Scientific research also has some illumination on this problem. Chronic unforgiveness causes stress. Every time people think of their transgressor, their body responds negatively. Decreasing your unforgiveness cuts down on your health risk. Now, if you can forgive, that can actually strengthen your immune system."

We have numerous testimonies of people who received their healing only by forgiving someone else. You can actually be tempted to think that their sickness was a mere pretention because it instantly disappeared together with the accompanying symptoms. Even doctors are left bewilded as such healing makes no sense in medical science.

In addition some children have been healed from life threatening sicknesses as their parents embraced forgiveness. It's becoming increasingly clear to me that in the spiritual realm, we open a door for the enemy to afflict us or our children when we hung onto unforgiveness. Many people who are exhausting their savings on medical treatment could find a cheaper and permanent solution through the avenue of forgiveness.

Unforgiveness is a path to self destruction

When you cannot tolerate the site of a certain person or people, your heart will always be troubled when you see or meet them. You will refuse to help even when in a position to and you may also miss some important opportunities in life.

Why give someone else the key to your happiness? That is exactly what some people have done. Their day to day happiness depends on whether they interact with certain person or not.

Hatred, anger and bitterness against a certain person or group of persons have never been an asset. It does not resolve any contentions we have and neither does it favour us in any way. In some instances the perceived offender has no idea of his offence or that he is hated that much. The political landscape is littered with such cases. I once was told of a woman who hated a certain politician with such passion that at the mention of his name she would puke. The worst was when he appeared on TV, just seeing his face alone was sufficient to trigger convulsions leading to hospitalization. I can assure you that she has never met the politician in question and most likely never will during her entire lifetime. She might die prematurely for somebody who doesn't know her and who has no ill feelings towards her.

Hatred is too big a burden for anyone to carry in this life. You can save yourself by choosing love over hatred as the Lord Jesus directed us to love our neighbors as ourselves (Matt 19:19). Interestingly the Lord did not stop there. He went on to issue an even higher standard of love by commanding us to love our enemies (Matt 5:43-44). So we really don't have any choice to hate people. The only way to live a fruitful life and enjoy the fruits of your labour peacefully is by loving.

Missing Heaven

Unfortunately, the worst consequence for unforgiveness is missing our eternal home in heaven. I discussed this in the introduction of this book. You don't want to miss heaven at any cost. Don't allow your offender to determine your eternal destiny. Simply put, Unforgiveness is a one way ticket to an eternity outside of God's paradise. Unbook yourself today by choosing to forgive all those who have offended you in any way. Forgive today for the sake of a better future, an eternity with God.

The scriptures below are very clear on what God's will is and represents His commands in the area of forgiveness.

Matt 5:43-45

43 "You have heard that it was said, "YOU SHALL LOVE YOUR NEIGHBOR and hate your enemy.'

44 "But I say to you, love your enemies and pray for those who persecute you,

45 so that you may be sons of your Father who is in heaven; for He causes His sun to rise on the evil and the good, and sends rain on the righteous and the unrighteous.

One of the manifest fruits of salvation is love for our enemies. If you can truly love your enemy, you qualify for the title born again. Failure to love our enemies is disobedience against the word of God and can lead us to be rejected by God.

Rom 12:19-21

19Do not take revenge, my dear friends, but leave room for God's wrath, for it is written: "It is mine to avenge; I will repay," says the Lord. 20On the contrary: "If your enemy is hungry, feed him; if he is thirsty, give him something to drink. In doing this, you will heap burning coals on his head." 21Do not be overcome by evil, but overcome evil with good.

While revenge against our enemies may sound like a splendid idea, it does not necessarily represent God's perfect will for us. He wants us to leave the battle to Him. At the very end you will appreciate that God knows how to deal with the wicked, and when he does, you will be left pleading for mercy.

Matt 18:32-35

32"Then the master called the servant in. 'You wicked servant,' he said, 'I canceled all that debt of yours because you begged me to. 33Shouldn't you have had mercy on your fellow servant just as I had on you?' 34In anger his master handed him over to the jailers to be tortured, until he should pay back all he owed. 35"This is how my heavenly Father will treat each of you unless you forgive a brother or sister from your heart."

Remember that if you are born again, God has cancelled in full your debt of sin. If you are not yet a believer in Christ, He is ready and willing to forgive you all your sins. All you need is to humble yourself and approach Him with a repentant heart, confess your sins and ask for forgiveness. You will be amazed at the results. He therefore commands and expects you to forgive others in the same breath. You cannot afford to miss heaven on account of someone who offended you. Forgive and let go.

Unforgiveness in the Last Days

These last days are indeed terrible. We hardly see the need to forgive others. The society is growing more and more hostile towards God's laws and regulations. National constitutions are being reviewed regularly to entrench ungodly human rights within the laws. We are becoming more materialistic and egocentric by the day. People are always looking for opportunities to take advantage of others and make more money. The scripture says;

You should also know this, Timothy, that in the last days there will be very difficult times. For people will love only themselves and their money. They will be boastful and proud, scoffing at God, disobedient to their parents, and ungrateful. They will consider nothing sacred. 3 They will be unloving and unforgiving; they will slander others and have no self-control; they will be cruel and have no interest in what is good. They will betray their friends, be reckless, be puffed up with pride, and love pleasure rather than God. They will act as if they are religious, but they will reject the power that could make them godly. You must stay away from people like that, 2 Tim 3:1-5.

When you review what is happening around the world today, there are clear signals that we are living in the last days. One of the clear signs, as prophesied by Paul the apostle, is that people will be unloving and unforgiving. This is well demonstrated for instance in the marriage covenant in which many people actually stopped honouring long time ago. Marriage has now become like a revolving door where you walk in and out at will. People, including Christians, no longer remember their vows to one another made before God. They stop loving their spouses and refuse to forgive each other. As a result we are seeing an all time high divorce rate which keeps on increasing every year. This is also supported by the new laws we have made for ourselves which have made divorce very easy and simple.

I have stated that without a forgiving heart, marriage is practically impossible. It is no longer uncommon to meet someone who has a fifth husband or wife, just like the Samaritan woman. They are searching for a perfect partner who will always do the right things and never require forgiveness. Of course we all know that such a spouse does not exist on planet earth and therefore these unforgiving people find themselves chasing the wind and never seem to catch up with it. All they need to do is ask God for a forgiving heart and choose to offer Forgivenes, Unlimited in their current relationships. If this happens they will never seek for any other divorce but will learn step by step, how to live with a fellow fallen human being, who is full of weaknesses and failures. Remember that all things are possible with God i.e. if we allow God to direct our lives.

In 2 Tim 3:5, we are actually warned to keep a distance from unloving and unforgiving people. They always want to show you how much they have been offended and show you why forgiving is impossible. If you hang around them long enough they might infect you with this deadly disease called unforgiveness. Don't allow it to happen to you. You have a better inheritance and more important issues to focus on and move forward in your life and relationship with God. It has been proven scientifically that no one can make good progress forward by walking or running when looking behind. Paul shows us the way in the passage below.

I don't mean to say that I have already achieved these things or that I have already reached perfection! But I keep working toward that day when I will finally be all that Christ Jesus saved me for and wants me to be, Phil. 3:12

God requires all of us to forgive unconditionally and forget. Unforgiveness is an unnecessary interruption on our journey and we must get rid of it immediately it rears its ugly head. It is a strange burden which is carried without any benefits at all. Otherwise we may end up going round and round the mountain like the Israelites without making any substantial progress on the spiritual front. There are things which God wants you to do but you may never manage to accomplish them unless you overcome unforgiveness. This is your day to say like Paul; forgetting the past, I will do my best to move forward and win the prize. I will be excited to meet you in the New Jerusalem, as one who overcame unforgiveness and made it to the Promised Land by God's grace.

Let us be like children, who even after being spanked by their parents, promptly forget and continue to relate with them as if nothing ever happened. You must have simple faith like that of a child, believing that God has your best interests at heart and will help you overcome every challenge in life including unforgiveness. You should always remember that forgiveness will bring eternal benefits to you while unforgiveness results in eternal losses. Choose today, the way of forgiveness.

CHAPTER 7
SIMPLE STEPS TO FORGIVENESS

1. Submit yourself to God

You will realize that it's difficult to extend forgiveness to others on your own. God will help you forgive because not only has He forgiven billions of people, He also has the power to help you, in particular. Just remember: He only helps those who admit their helplessness. You might say a simple prayer like this:

God I am finding it difficult to forgive (insert name) with my own power. Please Lord help me. Help me to understand how much You have forgiven me, so I can forgive the person who has hurt me. I ask this in Jesus name, Amen.

2. Acknowledge the wrong done to you

In the African tradition we have a proverb which states that once water has been poured out on the soil, it's impossible to get it back into the bucket. **You can't truly forgive unless you have grasped the extent of the violation that has been done against you.** With the help of a counselor, minister, or another professional, you need to seek to understand what happened to you when you were hurt and why it hurts so much. In other words Count the cost of what is owed to you.

Once you realize that you cannot undo the past wrongs done to you, then you discover that the most responsible way out of it is to accept that it happened, it was bad, it hurt and maybe altered something in our lives and/or relationships, it caused us to lose something, but thanks be to God we can do something about it.

Let all the things that have happened roll through your mind, and let them pass through. Don't try to deny feelings of anguish that you may have had. If you keep trying to smother that fire, you won't help it. Allow yourself to experience the feelings you need to go through, then don't cling to them, let them go.

Feeling bad and hating our offenders is an alternative route we can choose, but it will not be helpful to us. Even revenging will not obliterate the wrong or expunge it from our past. It might even make matters worse.

Also when we reflect on our past and recall how we have been forgiven by God for everything we have ever done, it is then that we are able to begin forgiving the people in our lives who have hurt us.

3. Choose to release the offender

Now it's time to make the big decision to surrender. Let go of your deep desire to get even with the person who offended you. Come up with a prayer or statement announcing your decision.

Here's an example: *By an act of my will, and God's grace, I give up my rights to get even with (insert name). I make a commitment that when those sordid feelings come over me again, I will release them. I won't babysit them. I admit the feelings are real, but I choose not to be controlled by them any longer. Instead I will dwell on the good things I have learned from this experience.*

- Sometimes God will lead you to speak forgiveness directly to the person who hurt you, which can lead to reconciliation. Most often, though, He just wants you to speak forgiveness out loud to Him, with the help of another friend, your small group, a counselor, or a pastor.

- Confess and repent of the judgments that you made against the person. Break the vows in the name of Jesus. Vows are spiritual strongholds of the soul. Your prayer partner or small group can join you, praying that God would undo the power that a vow has had over your life.

- Identify the lies that you believed because you got hurt. Ask God to replace the lie with the truth. Again, your prayer partner or group can join you in this process.

4. Make a choice to have compassion on your offender

Look at them first, as a tragedy. In one sense they should be pitied. Bottom line is, because of their violation against you they have suffered, are suffering, and in the end will suffer far more in this life, or the one to come. The law of planting and reaping is still in force (Gal 6:7-8)

We're not making excuses for them, but we're only saying they are pathetic, and desperately need our compassion. One way to show compassion is to pray for the person who has hurt you. Jesus said, *"Pray for your enemies."* He knows it is impossible to continue to pray for someone, and still hate them. Then, while you're praying for this person, ask for a blessing in their life. Pray that good things come to them. Wish them well.

If the offender is alive and approachable, you can let them know that you have forgiven them. You could also call, or send a text message, a letter or email to let them know that you no longer hold ill feelings towards them. Your counselor or minister can help you choose the mode of communication depending on the circumstances.

In this way you will be releasing yourself from a bondage which threatens your relationships, your life and your eternal destiny.

4 important persons who should be forgiven

1. The Offender

Obviously the person responsible for hurting you requires your forgiveness. He or she is part of the fallen human race who deserves to be pitied as we have already discussed.

Remember that forgiveness does not excuse the behavior but prevents the behavior from negatively affecting us

2. Offenders friends/sympathizers

Secondly, probably your offender has friends or relatives who cheered them on and supported them in their wicked actions against you. You should also extend forgiveness to them.

When you forgive you are doing yourself a favour which no one else can do for you.

3. Self

The 3rd person who needs forgiveness is yourself. Often times we hold ourselves responsible for what happened to us, which could be true or not. This may keep us regretting and wishing we never involved ourselves in a particular situation, transaction or relationship. Of course with the wisdom of hindsight we should choose to be more careful in future and avoid similar offences coming to us. But for your own benefit, you need to accept your mistakes, learn the lessons, forgive yourself and move on with life. You don't benefit by crying over spilt milk all the days of your life.

You should not allow yourself to be detained by you past. Self-forgiveness is an important step in our healing process. Internal healing enables us to take care of our external circumstances.

4. God

Now this is an interesting one and some people will be asking why and how we should even think of forgiving God. Strange as it may sound to you, in reality there are many people who blame God for allowing bad things to happen to them or their families while he actually has the power to stop it. Well, its true God could have stopped it, but in His infinite wisdom He allowed it to happen. It is practically impossible for us to fully understand the mind of God.

*Isaiah 40[28]Have you not known? Have you not heard? The everlasting God, the Lord, the Creator of the ends of the earth, does not faint or grow weary; **there is no searching of His understanding.***

You may strongly feel that God failed to live up to your expectations. The devil would really love to have you linger there for quite a long time. In this way he keeps you blinded from seeing the great things God has done or is doing in your life and around you. This attitude also keeps you from seeking God's help and thereby missing blessings.

Surely, you don't want to be bitter and resentful towards God. Most of all, you don't want your relationship with God to become strained. So, even though you don't understand why He did not intervene in your circumstances, just choose to forgive God for letting you down and live in peace because of it. In fact, as you do this, you will start feeling more connected to God than ever before.

Spiritual Warfare

You will be required to wage war against the enemy of your soul. He is aware that you now know the truth and can almost predict your next course of action. You will win the war through consistent and persistent prayer.

1 Peter 5:8 Admonishes us to '*Be careful! Watch out for attacks from the Devil, your great enemy. He prowls around like a roaring lion, looking for some victim to devour,*'

The Devil is not your friend. He does not have your welfare in mind. He looks for every opportunity to keep you in bondage and ensure that you don't enjoy God's blessings. This time round, don't allow yourself to become his victim. We all know the three fold mission of the enemy as spelt out by the Lord Jesus in John 10:10; *The thief cometh not, but for to steal, and to kill, and to destroy: I am come that they might have life, and that they might have it more abundantly.*

Your enemy has been more than happy to keep you in the prison of unforgiveness all these years. He is now very disturbed that you have known the truth and that you are now intending to obey God's word and release yourself from prison. He will therefore try by all means to block you in all manner of ways. His intention is to steal your joy and peace and if possible to kill and destroy you through hatred, anger and bitterness. Don't pay any attention to his words for he is a liar. The devil lied to Eve and caused both her and the husband to be expelled from God's presence. His tricks are still the same today and will be applied even in the matter of forgiveness. You will hear a voice whispering to you things like these:

"Does God really require us to forgive?", What do you think you are doing?", this is real madness, surely you must be more clever than this. How can you allow yourself to be trampled on like a doormat?"

Remember this is the same old devil whose pleasure is to see you walking contrary to God's will and thereafter suffering the attendant consequences. So what should you do? Resist the enemy steadfastly. James 4:7-8 says that we should humble ourselves before God. Resist the Devil, and he will flee from us.

You must make it your daily business to resist the enemy and he will flee from you. Don't entertain his nonsensical arguments. Immerse yourself deep in God's word and choose to listen to God continually. Let God's word shape your perspectives in life. Live by the word and you will indeed be more than a conqueror. That is your lot in life. That is what Christ died for, to make you a winner, always. Don't settle for anything less.

CHAPTER 8
PRAYER GUIDE

In this section I have included a short prayer guide to help you pray for deliverance from the shackles of unforgiveness. Please use it in addition to all other points the Holy Spirit will drop into your heart. You can also seek the help of your prayer partner or your local pastor as you wage battle on this front.

Who has believed our message? To whom will the LORD reveal his saving power? Isa. 53:1

- Pray that the Holy Spirit will help you to believe God's report. Pray that God will deliver you from the spirit of doubt and unbelief.

Luke 1:45: You are blessed, because you believed that the Lord would do what he said."

- Your blessings and happiness is directly dependent on believing God's word. Pray that you will experience the blessing of taking God at His word.

Josh 1:8 says that we study this Book of the Law continually, meditate on it day and night so you may be sure to obey all that is written in it. Only then will we succeed.

- Pray that you will join the company of those who study the word continually.

- Pray for grace to meditate upon the word daily and to obey it fully.

The Bible says, We who have the Spirit understand these things, but others can't understand us at all. How could they? For, "Who can know what the Lord is thinking? Who can give him counsel?" But we can understand these things, for we have the mind of Christ, 1Cor 2:15-16.

- Pray that God will give you the mind of Christ to enable you accept the things of God at face value without any resistance.

Ps 139:23-24: Search me, O God, and know my heart; test me and know my thoughts. Point out anything in me that offends you, and lead me along the path of everlasting life.

- Ask God to search your heart and reveal every area in which you may be harboring hatred, bitterness and/or unforgiveness.

- Pray that God will bring to light every form of hypocrisy in your life and help you overcome it.

- Pray that God will lead you on the path of forgiveness giving you grace to walk patiently along it with Him.

Isa 43:25: I, even I, am he that blotteth out thy transgressions for mine own sake, and will not remember thy sins.

- Remember you are a son of God and therefore God's nature is woven into your fabric. You have the right to emulate your father in the area of forgiveness. Pray that God will enable you to sincerely forgive and forget.

The Bible says, The Spirit of the Lord is upon me, because he hath anointed me to preach the gospel to the poor; he hath sent me to heal the brokenhearted, to preach deliverance to the captives, and recovering of sight to the blind, to set at liberty them that are bruised, Luke 4:18.

- Ask God to set you free from the bondage of unforgiveness.

- Pray that you will become a role model in the area of forgiveness and that many will follow your example.

- Pray that you will become a teacher on the subject of forgiveness and help deliver many from the prison of unforgiveness.

- Command the evil spirit of unforgiveness to depart from your life forever.

The Bible says, Blessed are ye, when men shall revile you, and persecute you, and shall say all manner of evil against you falsely, for my sake. Rejoice, and be exceeding glad: for great is your reward in heaven: for so persecuted they the prophets which were before you, Matt 5:11-12

- Pray that God will enable you to rejoice in the midst of all the trouble or persecution you may be suffering presently.

Rom 8:18: For I reckon that the sufferings of this present time are not worthy to be compared with the glory which shall be revealed in us.

- Pray that God will give you a vision of heaven. With this revelation you will be able to rejoice in your sufferings, seeing the glory awaiting you in heaven.

The Bible says, "You have heard that the law of Moses says, 'Love your neighbor' and hate your enemy. 44 But I say, love your enemies! Pray for those who persecute you! 45 In that way, you will be acting as true children of your Father in heaven. For he gives his sunlight to both the evil and the good, and he sends rain on the just and on the unjust, too, Matt 5:43-46.

- Ask God to deposit in your heart true love for your enemies.

- Ask God for grace to pray for the salvation of your enemies. Remember Jesus died for them also.

The LORD says, "I will give you back what you lost to the stripping locusts, the cutting locusts, the swarming locusts, and the hopping locusts. It was I who sent this great destroying army against you, Joel 2:25-26.

- Pray for the restoration of all you have lost in the years you walked in ignorance, hating people and being hated.

- Ask God to heal you from, every sickness that came to you through the opened door of unforgiveness.

- Pray for restoration of relationships with loved ones, colleagues in your place of work, other believers and ministry partners.

But the LORD will have mercy on the descendants of Jacob. Israel will be his special people once again. He will bring them back to settle once again in their own land. And people from many different nations will come and join them there and become a part of the people of Israel, Isa 14:1-2.

- Pray that God will once again restore you onto the path of your prophetic destiny.

- Pray that the gifts and callings of God upon your life will be restored once again.

- Pray that God will help you to start making considerable and tangible progress in every area of your life.

The Bible says, Arise, Jerusalem! Let your light shine for all the nations to see! For the glory of the LORD is shining upon you, Isa 60:1-2.

- Pray that God will restore His glory upon you and make you shine in your generation.

- Pray that God will make you a blessing to others beyond any of your imaginations

And now, all glory to God, who is able to keep you from stumbling, and who will bring you into his glorious presence innocent of sin and with great joy, Jude 24

- Pray that at the appearing of the Lord Jesus Christ, you will be found blameless and spotless before God.

May the Lord Jesus, who paid the full price for your freedom, set you free from unforgiveness, indeed

To forgive is to set a prisoner free and discover that the prisoner was you.— Lewis B. Smedes. 1

The weak can never forgive. Forgiveness is the attribute of the strong. Mahatma Gandhi 2

To forgive is the highest, most beautiful form of love. In return, you will receive untold peace and happiness. Robert Muller 3

Always forgive your enemies; nothing annoys them so much. — Oscar Wilde. 4

Forgiveness is almost a selfish act because of its immense benefits to the one who forgives.— Lawana Blackwell. 5

Forgiveness is a gift you give to yourself. It is not something you do FOR someone else.— Larry James. 6

Notes:

1. http://www.brainyquote.com/quotes/topics/topic_forgiveness.html

2. http://www.brainyquote.com/quotes/topics/topic_forgiveness.html

3. http://thinkexist.com/quotations/forgiveness/

4. http://www.quotationspage.com/subjects/forgiveness/

5.http://www.quotationspage.com/subjects/forgiveness/

6. http://www.celebratelove.com/forgive.htm

Printed in the United States
by Baker & Taylor Publisher Services